Give Comfort
to
My People

Give Comfort
to
My People

by
Joseph M. Dolan

PAULIST PRESS
New York/Ramsey/Toronto

Library of Congress
Catalog Card Number: 77-80804

ISBN: 0-8091-2037-2

Published by Paulist Press
Editorial Office: 1865 Broadway, New York, N.Y. 10023
Business Office: 545 Island Road, Ramsey, N.J. 07446

Printed and bound in the
United States of America

Contents

vi   CONTENTS

Preface

"All of you are Christ's body, and each one has a part in it" (1 Cor. 12:27). To understand ourselves as a Church is to realize ourselves as truly the body of the Lord Jesus. We speak of the Church as mission, as pilgrim, as called forth, as sent, as teacher, as prophet, and as service. Not to experience ourselves as a people bound to each other by the Spirit of love and sharing the common life of the Lord Jesus is to fall short of realizing ourselves as the growing, dynamic Church we truly are.

Jesus lives now. He lives in and through us. It is he who sends us forth to free and heal and make whole our brothers and sisters. An awareness of this fact gives direction and vitality to the pastoral care of the sick, elderly and handicapped. Each one of us is part of his body. We all take part in serving and being served. When we serve others, we are served in return. This is the dynamic. Jesus serves his body in his way, not ours. We seek to discern the Lord's touch, not ours.

The team approach to the sick and elderly described in this book is the result of an experience. It is an experience that was conceived in prayer, nurtured by doing and born of the Spirit through reflection upon the experience. A team approach involves the gifts of priests, religious, and laity working together in the blending of ministries. Each person in the body of Jesus uses his or her gifts for others. The salvation of the

Lord is accomplished as we in his body serve each other, each one of us using our gifts and ministering to each other whether we are priests, religious, or laity. We are a Jesus-centered Church. Salvation comes through a blending of our ministries. Loving one another means serving each other. It is a dying to and for each other that we truly live and give life.

My experience of shared ministry began a few years ago after I had been appointed the Director of the Office for the Pastoral Care of the Sick in Catholic Charities in the diocese of Brooklyn, New York. I had served as hospital chaplain for five years. As director, administrative duties occupied most of my time. I missed visiting and ministering to the sick. I mentioned this to a friend, Sister Julie Houser, C.S.J., a teacher at Our Lady of Snows School in North Floral Park. I told her that I felt a need to go at least once a week to a hospital. She decided to visit with me, and so began what has been developed in this book. We prayed together, asking the Spirit to help us choose a hospital. After visiting two hospitals we decided upon LaGuardia Hospital in Forest Hills, New York. The hospital was a HIP hospital and had a cross-section of people from throughout the city. The priests of the local parish were stretched thin serving two hospitals and three nursing homes, so we decided that this was a place which could use some help.

Sister Julie and I met each Monday afternoon before the Blessed Sacrament in Our Lady Queen of Martyrs Church. We felt that the Eucharist should be brought from the local parish church. Before going to the hospital we prayed to Jesus to use us in whatever way he wished, and to lead us to those whom he wished to free from whatever he so wished. We literally asked Jesus to take us to the hospital and use us, and he truly did. He used us to bring people to himself in ways I had not experienced before. People who for years had been away from the sacraments received them once more. It was a common experience to witness the power of the Lord's love as he touched people to free them physically, spiritually, and emotionally. We made a prayer list of specific people with specific needs. These we prayed for during the week, lifting them and their needs to the Lord. It seemed that to the extent that we prayed, the next week's visit bore the fruit of which the Lord spoke. We began visiting at two o'clock in the afternoon and finished about eight o'clock in the evening. After a morning at the office and school, it was a long day, but what was happening and what the Lord was teaching made it all worthwhile.

After about six months, Sister Marie Lenihan, Sister Nazaire Duhamel and Sister Patricia Murphy, all Josephite Sisters and teachers at St. Pascal Baylon's High School, joined us. We were now five. All the sisters became extraordinary ministers of the Eucharist.

We were learning a blending of ministries and a team approach to the sick. The Lord was using each of us in our own uniqueness. We were now able to finish our four-hundred-bed hospital in about three hours.

A year later, Father Francis Mulhall, the Administrator of Our Lady Queen of Martyrs, after consultation with his associates, hired Sister Marie Lenihan as a Pastoral Associate to manage the Pastoral Ministry to two hospitals, three nursing homes in the parish, and the shut-ins. Seventy-five parishioners are now part of the pastoral care team. They pray together and serve their brothers and sisters in the dynamic described in this book.

The same pastoral care team approach has been established in many parishes in the diocese and is spreading, but training of those who serve as part of the team and those who manage the team is essential. A system of continuing education and supervision is also essential to a successful diocesan-wide program.

Pastors and parish priests will find this book informative in setting up and maintaining a pastoral care program for those in their parishes, whether at home or in a hospital or nursing home. The flexibility of the program permits a response to whatever need is present in the parish. Parish priests will find it especially useful as a textbook to use in training the pastoral ministers and managers of the pastoral team.

Seminarians, religious and laity with little or no experience with the sick and elderly will find it extremely informative. It can easily be used as a primer in pastoral care for those beginning in the work. Diocesan Coordinators of Pastoral Care would find the contents especially helpful in programming a diocesan effort to reach the needy of the diocese through local community response and management.

To truly become a community, Christians must become a faith community sensitive to and aware of Jesus present among them in the lives of their suffering brothers and sisters.

The frightened sick man is Jesus stretching out his hand to grasp ours as we prayerfully approach his altar of pain and suffering. The friendless, isolated and lonely elderly woman in her tenement flat is Jesus as she stares at the door hoping someone will knock, even someone looking for someone else. The thirty-five-year-old spastic girl is Jesus as she spends day after day looking for a kind word and acceptance of herself as a unique person who is lovable, or looking perhaps just for someone to trust. The young child awake all night suffering from hunger pains is Jesus. The young man on the dialysis machine is Jesus as he passes hour after hour in dependency so that he may live. Jesus is sick, elderly, handicapped, retarded, addicted, imprisoned, delinquent, troubled in mind and body—our brother and sister, Jesus. "As often as you did it for one of my least brothers, you did it for me" (Mt. 25:40).

Our mission is a commitment to service. We are, through baptism and confirmation, a people summoned and sent forth to serve. We must reach out our hands to our brothers and sisters in the body of the Lord.

We must truly become a compassionate and loving community of believers. We must be eager to sacrifice, ready to suffer and to stretch out our arms to embrace our brothers and sisters as Jesus sacrifices and suffers in them.

To my suffering brothers and sisters who through their response to the Lord in their trials have taught me to experience a living Lord who touches our lives in love, I dedicate this book.

May the Lord Jesus be praised!

1
Toward a Theology of Pastoral Team Ministry

To be truly pastoral, a theology must say something of the nature of the Church, the persons served and the persons serving. A pastoral theology finds its expression from the experience of a person as he accepts the touch of God freeing him, healing him, and making him whole.

First we must speak about the nature of the Church. The Church is by its nature a people called together by the Holy Spirit. It is a gathering together of a people into community in the unity of their uniquenesses. With Jesus as the head of his body, we gather together one in faith, one in baptism, one in love. It is a sharing in the one Lord, one salvation, one freedom. The Church is the visible Jesus in our world. As members of Jesus' body, we are engaged in an intimate personal relationship with the Lord. The relationship is so intimate that the members, open to the action of the Holy Spirit, are in the process of becoming what the Lord has willed for each member. Without destroying the uniqueness of each person or in any way diminishing his nature, Jesus touches the lives of his members in so intimate a way that they form together with him one body, the Church, imbued and permeated with God's divine life.

The members of Jesus' body, although separate and distinct, are possessed by him so intimately that the more they respond to his Spirit touching their lives, the more they radiate Jesus in their daily living; they begin to put on the mind of Jesus, seeing things as he sees them, hearing things as he hears them, and speaking with the power of his words, touching with his hands, walking with his feet, and loving as he loves. It is a way of experiencing the risen Jesus by dying and rising with him through baptism and confirmation and the daily living out of this commitment. It is in the awareness of this intimacy with the Lord that a member of Jesus' body experiences his loving touch in his life and allows Jesus to use him to free others.

Jesus frees, heals, and makes people whole through us. It is we who carry the power of his cross and resurrection, his freedom and salvation to others. This is the nature of the Church—to bring man to the Father by worshiping him and serving each other through Jesus, our Savior and brother, by the power and love of his Spirit.

Second, we must say something about the persons served. The Lord wants all of us to be whole. This is the meaning of salvation. Jesus came to set us free, to give to those who believe in him a share in his divine life by bringing us to wholeness. We speak so much about saving souls, but it is we who are saved. It is the person who must be set free. It is the person who is saved by Jesus. We must be open to the working of the Lord within the person to whom we are ministering. People are not free. They are bound up in tombs of their own making such as prejudices, fears, anxieties, hatreds, pride, lust and the whole gamut of human problems which accompany sickness and growing old.

The spectrum of the human condition finds its expression in peoples of all ages. Many times it is only accentuated when the person became sick, elderly, or handicapped.

For example, when someone has a gall bladder attack, it is the person who becomes sick, not the gall bladder. The gall bladder is diseased. The person is sick. The disease affects the entire person, physically, psychologically, emotionally, and spiritually. Then he turns to the God in whom he believes, to bring him back into harmony by freeing him from this sickness and its effects upon his person and to make him whole. He believes that through those who serve him—doctors, nurses, minister, and hospital staff—and those who support him in his time of trial—his family, friends, and neighbors—God will bring him to wholeness again.

Finally we must speak about the persons serving. Wholeness becomes a reality through the ministry of those serving. Jesus serves his body through the ministry of a praying and concerned community. The pastoral minister is also in the process of becoming. He has not arrived; he is arriving. He must see himself as a pilgrim, as on a journey with his brothers and sisters. He must be aware of himself as someone whom the Lord uses to free his brothers or sisters. The pastoral minister doesn't save anyone. Jesus does. That is why the minister must open himself to the action of the Spirit in his own life. He must live in total trust and total confidence in the Lord. He must see himself as a cooperator in the new creation the Lord is accomplishing in himself and those he serves.

The ministry of the priest is a commission which touches the essence of his orders. He cannot lay claim to the fullness of who he is unless he responds, when called upon, to minister to his brothers and sisters when in need. To isolate or segregate himself from those who suffer would be to deny the healing Jesus himself.

The priest must take the initiative in bringing to the attention of his fellow Christians the command of Jesus that we love one another. He has the duty to call forth in the hearts of those he serves a generous response and reaching out to his neighbor.

The need to come together in order to experience each other as members of Jesus' body and the resultant awareness that we are our brother's keeper are essential to his ministry. Jesus commands us to love each other. We cannot be a disciple unless we do just that.

The sick, for example, are freed from sickness through medical care. The ministry of doctors using their God-given talents and skills, the drugs, the medical procedure, the medical team working together—all are simply the continuation of the redemption of the Lord Jesus' struggle against the evils which plague man. It is through God's providence and God's power made manifest in the talents, skills, and gifts of our fellow man that we are freed and healed and made whole.

All Christians have a real part in that struggle. This is ministry—each with his God-given talents and gifts, using them not for his own ends but for the service of others.

The priest ministers to the needy by bringing Jesus' freeing and healing touch in his sacraments and through the sacrament of his own presence among them.

Religious bring to the needy the dedicated and self-less presence of Jesus manifested and witnessed in their own lives and the comfort that their Church, their Jesus, has not forgotten them.

The laity in ministry fulfill their baptismal and confirmation promises to love God and neighbor and to reach out to the suffering Jesus in the person of their neighbors.

Ministry must involve all Christians—priests, religious, and laity joined in prayer, under the guidance of the Spirit, serving Jesus in his brothers and sisters for the honor and glory of the Father.

2
The Parish:
Alive and Reaching Out

Ten percent of the parishioners in an average parish are homebound—shut-ins, sick, aging, handicapped. A parish truly wishing to reach all of its people will of necessity have to elicit a response from the total Christian community. The greatest challenge is to find those people who somehow have dropped out of sight. They have melted into the crowd, become lost, disappeared. No one notices them or even sees them. They spend their days, months, years without a word, or perhaps only a few remarks with the neighborhood grocer each morning, if they can go out. They are our forgotten parishioners. They are our brothers and sisters for whom isolation, poverty, loneliness, fear and depression have become a way of life. Not too many people really care.

If our institutionalized sick, elderly and handdicapped are not too often considered parishioners, their counterparts living at home are even more neglected by the Christian community. At least we know those in our institutions. They are identifiable. But half of the people who live at home live alone or with non-relatives. Most are unknown.

A parish program should address itself to both

groups of people, those who come to church for programs and those who cannot come or do not come to church programs.

Those who come to church programs are the people who attend the golden age clubs, belong to societies, come to community senior citizen centers, attend programs for the handicapped, and by and large receive help with their many problems.

These programs merely touch the tip of the iceberg. Although very fine programs, they reach only a small segment of the people out there. How do we reach them? And what do we do when we reach them?

I believe that a parish must first begin by having a vision of itself as a people. This may sound basic, but too many parishes do not see themselves this way. Parishes are looked upon, spoken about and seen by onlookers as buildings—the "plant."

We have too much of a tendency and tradition of viewing our parishes as the rectory and its buildings. The physical plant becomes the Church. So the programs we initiate do not include our brothers and sisters who do not come or cannot come to the buildings.

We have not only cut out of our ministry the institutionalized sick, elderly and handicapped, or limited the ministry to them as infrequently as possible, but we have built our church buildings with steps and barriers which keep even willing sick, elderly and handicapped parishioners from coming inside. They must go to special places where the barriers do not exist. We often wonder: "Where did all the children go?" Let us not forget that the elderly are also God's children.

Reaching out to our forgotten brothers and sisters is the obligation of all the people of God—the Christian community. The priest cannot and is not expected to do it alone. He can't. The volume of people is too great, and the problems are too many.

The parish will begin to realize itself as a community only when it begins to truly pray together. This is essential. I do not mean that someone says a prayer at the opening of a meeting, or that we pray at Sunday worship a prayer of the faithful for the success of parish programs. I mean praying together in a prayer of praise, thanksgiving, adoration and petition. I mean prayer that involves those coming together, prayer that involves their daily living, prayer that involves the Lord as a reality in their lives. I mean prayer that truly recognizes Jesus as Lord of their lives and therefore Lord of all that is happening in the parish.

Without this awareness of prayer as a vehicle of growth and as essential to forming true community, the parish will always remain an organization, never an organism. Prayer of this nature makes the parish a source of healing. It makes the parish the focus of the freeing power of the Lord Jesus.

It is not our usual style. In most parishes it is not a reality. It requires time for people to come together for prayer alone. So many meetings we have in our parishes seem to get God out of the way by saying a "short prayer" before we get down to our "real" agenda. We say that God is the real power in our parishes, but we act as if we were. We ask the Father to "give us this day our daily bread," but we act as if we earned it. We wonder why our yoke is difficult and our burdens terribly heavy. Could it be that we rely too much on our own power? The Lord told us that his yoke was easy and his burden light. When we rely on the Lord's power and not ours, this is very true. Sometimes I think the reason why we fall flat on our faces is that we rely way too much on ourselves and not enough on the Lord. "Seek first the Kingdom of God and all things will be added unto you" (Lk. 12:31).

To realize ourselves as a people, as pastoral ministers, as the body of Lord, we must become one in the Spirit. Only then can we begin to touch people's lives with the touch of the Lord. It is more important to gather together around the Lord than to gather together around a task.

Our coming together must be to discern what the Lord wants us to do in building his Kingdom in this parish. So many plans we have seem to go nowhere. I believe it is because these plans are not the Lord's. They may be merely the pastor's idea, not the Lord's plan. Perhaps the idea of the presidents of the rosary and altar societies is not the Lord's plan. Perhaps it is the Lord's plan for another parish but not for this one; plans for one parish often do not "work" in another. I believe the Lord is telling us to pray to discern his plan for us, here, now, in this place, and for this people.

3
Jesus of the Moment

Touching people's lives is much more than a few hellos, a handshake, living next door, being on a parish council. It means a face-to-face encounter; it means a sharing, getting to know each other, experiencing each other's presence. It is making Jesus present.

Climb to the top of a mountain, take off your shoes and walk in the grass, scratch your back on a tree, walk in the sand in your bare feet, close your eyes and listen to the sounds of the ocean, go into the deep forest and listen to nature speaking, stand silent in the midst of mountain peaks and hear them shout, go into the depths of the earth and let the stillness touch your being.

We begin to experience God when we let him touch us. All of the beauties of nature that surround us speak to us of God only when we let them touch us. We can look at mountains and yet never truly see them. Only when they speak to us and touch us do they share their beauty with us.

People are very much like the rest of God's creations. We never really share their beauty until we let them come close enough to touch us. We keep people at a distance by our defenses.

We have so many fears, attitudes, prejudices. We can't afford to let people really know what we are truly like. Yet deep inside all of us are so many, many hungers that cry out to each other: "Look at me! Touch me! Love me!" This is our commonality. Jesus knew this. Jesus is one of us. Jesus had the same hungers. Jesus experienced loneliness, fear, anxiety, anger, disappointment. He knew what was in the human heart. Sometimes I think God became one of us so that he could experience what it was like to be human.

Joan experienced the human Jesus in her moment of need. Joan is very pretty, dresses well, takes a real pride in her appearance, is outgoing and very helpful to everyone around her. She wasn't always this way. I entered her life about a year and a half ago. She had been placed in a nursing home by her daughter.

She was a very confused lady, well into her eighties. Her excessive weight was accentuated by clothes which had become too tight for her. Her hair was disheveled, her stockings had fallen down around her ankles and shoes. When she smiled, it ended with a frown and a look which seemed to say "Do you really care or are you mouthing words when you ask me how I truly am?"

We learned from the administration and medical team that Joan was seeing a psychiatrist twice a week but nothing seemed to help. She did not respond to anything. Sister Julie and I spoke about her many times. We prayed for her specifically. We asked the Lord to teach us how to help her. Many other people began praying for her. The nuns in Sister Julie's convent included her in prayer. Sister Julie even collected some clothes from the other sisters and gave them to her. Her condition changed a bit but not completely. The dramatic change came when Jesus touched her heart and freed her from the emptiness of not being no-

ticed, of a sense of feeling that no one really cared
about her. If no one cared, why bother?

I met her coming down on the elevator one day
after she had gotten her daily dose of Librium. We
spoke a few minutes and then I knew that I must say to
her what I truly felt. I simply said, "Joan, please don't
get offended but I must tell you that you must have
been a very beautiful woman when you were young.
You are still very pretty, wrinkles here and there, but
very pretty. Why have you let yourself go? I would
truly love to see you get dressed up. You'd be a knock-
out." She just looked at me.

Within a week she had her hair set, began to wear
clothes that fit, put herself together. She has begun to
take off weight and has become a new person. Jesus
told us to learn from him because he was meek and
gentle of heart. I know what he means. Joan is an example of his touch. Love does change lives.

We become a community when we begin to realize
ourselves as a people, when we encounter each other in
the spirit of brotherhood and sisterhood. As long as we
remain in our parishes isolated from each other, we will
never become a community. Community presupposes a
sharing, and if we never get to know each other, how
can we even begin to share.

The priest must bring the people together; he must
be a convener. Like Jesus he must bring people together, let them realize each other in face to face encounters, urge them to pray together, know each other,
serve each other. We come together as the body of
Jesus. It isn't the things we do that bring us together
and form us into a people. It is the Lord Jesus and
what we are becoming that bring us together. The
parish is where the Kingdom is built. It is the place
where the people of God realize themselves as a com-

munity of believers, a people who love and care for each other because they are brothers and sisters of the Lord Jesus.

Every member of the parish has a gift given to him by God, a gift to be used in the service of his brother or sister. He has, in a word, a ministry which only he can give, a ministry to a neighbor which will never be done if he does not do it. This is how he will be judged by God to the measure that he serves his brothers and sisters, to the measure that he cares. The measure of our love of God is the measure of the love we have for the person we love the least. Jesus is constantly telling us that to be truly his followers we must serve each other. A pastoral care team in a parish will provide a vehicle so that this all may begin to happen.

The pastoral person who reaches out to his brother or sister in his need makes Jesus present in that relationship. In his reaching out he brings the touch of the Lord to the situation. Saint Francis lived in this reality which became his prayer of the moment.

Prayer of St. Francis

Lord, make me an instrument of your peace.
Where there is hatred, let me sow love;
where there is injury, pardon;
where there is doubt, faith;
where there is darkness, light;
and where there is sadness, joy.

O Divine Master, grant that I may not so much seek
to be consoled as to console;
to be understood, as to understand;
to be loved as to love.

For it is in giving that we receive,
it is in pardoning that we are pardoned,
And it is in dying that we are born to eternal life.

For Francis this was the Jesus of the moment. It was his coming together with his brother and sister in need that dispelled the darkness, satisfied the human hunger, filled the moment with light, made the moment Spirit-filled.

This is the dynamic of our relationships with those we reach out to serve—realizing that it is Jesus who is freeing, healing, making whole, and using us to bring the human need unfilled into his presence so that it may be touched by his love, a love that transforms us from persons performing tasks into vehicles of grace, power-centered in the Lord.

It is said that in New York City there are twelve million people with twelve million stories. This is one of those stories in which the Lord became present and dispelled the darkness in an elderly Jewish man's life. Somehow I feel God touched him specially. He had been a teacher "in his day." He had taught in a university, done special work teaching the mentally retarded, designed and produced from scraps a complete set of working tools for arts and crafts, and made molds from sheet metal so that he could teach the blind.

Up until a few years ago he visited the pediatric ward in a New York hospital each week. Many hours he spent entertaining children with his magic tricks. Now he is old, forgetful and very lonely. He receives very few visitors. He walks the corridors of a nursing home from morning to evening. All he has is memories —beautiful memories, but memories nonetheless. But what good is just remembering when you do not have anyone with whom to share those memories. Abe needed just that, someone to be interested in what he wanted to give and share.

The pastoral care team that visits his nursing home provided the vehicle for the Lord to touch him through those who visit. I am not quite sure whether they visit Abe or Abe visits them. He sometimes entertains the children who visit with his bag of tricks and is talking about helping blind children again someday. Perhaps Abe is coming out of himself. At least he's coming alive and has a lot of living yet to do.

There is a power that is released when two gather in the Lord's name. Do I believe this when I minister? Do I believe that my brother or sister who needs me is Jesus in my life? If we all truly believed it, our ministry would be on fire.

4
Calling Forth a People
and Growing into His Body

Most organizations are formed and function around the doing of a task. Our parishes were organized in this way. Parish societies were organized around needs. Societies were formed for the poor, for care of the altar, to usher at Mass, to run bingo, for teenagers, for young adults, for the elderly. For the most part societies are formed for the purpose of taking care of specific needs. Many of these societies spend hours trying to attract new members, as if great numbers were a sign of success. A great many societies are formed just to serve their membership, not to reach beyond the membership.

I am not suggesting that such parish societies should not be formed. The needs are real, and the people servicing them are performing a vital service to the Church. Yet it is not this type of organization that is being advocated here. We do not need just another parish society to meet the needs of the sick, elderly and handicapped. We need much more than that. What is being proposed is a coming together of men and women in the parish around their brother Jesus, realizing that when they come together they make him present, so that they may experience each other as brothers and sisters in his body. Through this coming together in prayer they discern the Lord's plan for his body in this parish. This can only be accomplished in prayer together. The people themselves create the body. His work accomplished through them touches the lives of those in the parish who are in need. I am suggesting the building of the church in the dynamic of Jesus. The parish is providing its people with opportunities to exercise ministries in the service of others. It is providing opportunities for people to use their unique gifts in the service of the Lord. They offer them to the Lord to be used. He will show them in the body where and with whom they are to share them.

The Christian comes together with his brothers and sisters to pray and learn from the Lord what is expected of him. I am reminded of the story in the Gospel of the young man who ran up to Jesus, knelt down in front of him and asked what he must do to gain eternal life. Jesus looked at him with love and told him: "You must go, sell what you have, give to the poor and follow me" (Mt. 19:21). That was what he had to do, but he went away sad, for he had many possessions. Sometimes I feel that this same story applies to many of us who are rich in time, but when Jesus asks us to give away some of it in the service of others and perhaps someone in particular, we walk away sad.

Bringing people together that they may realize themselves as a people of God, aware of themselves as Church, is the first step in the dynamic which must begin to happen among them. They must begin to see themselves not as isolated people helping out but as a people under the direction of the Spirit of Jesus guiding his body as it grows. They must be given the opportunity to experience each other, to see the beauty in each of the members and the oneness of Spirit that leads them to love one another. "The body is one and has many members, but all the members, many though they are, are one body, and so it is with Christ" (1 Cor. 12:12).

Pastoral ministers must realize, from the very beginning, that they have not been gathered together for the purpose of performing a function of visiting the sick, the aging, or the handicapped. They have been gathered together primarily to realize themselves as a community of believers. Only after they understand themselves as believers in the Lord Jesus and as his body in this world can they even begin to understand themselves as a people who are called forth to minister. That is exactly who they are—a people called forth under the guidance of the Spirit, aware of a special call, anointed to a task that only this particular person with a unique gift can do. I believe that Jesus uses each one of us specifically with certain people, and that he touches and saves them only through us. He uses our gift, our talent, our presence to make him present in the life of the person we have been sent forth to minister to.

We are, therefore, called forth from the Christian community to minister to our brothers and sisters. If our special gift or gifts are with the sick, aging, or handicapped, then we should step forward to become a pastoral minister to those people. If our special gift or gifts are with children or teaching, then we should step forward to become part of a pastoral team who would minister to the children as a teacher in the C.C.D. What is being said here could readily be applied to any ministry in the parish. Sometimes people discover a hidden gift in themselves only after they step forward to minister. The Lord seems to let us realize the great power that is within each of us once we are willing to trust him and ask him to lead where he wills.

The Lord Jesus selected and sent forward others to

spread the Kingdom. "The Lord appointed a further seventy-two and sent them in pairs before him to every town and place he intended to visit. He said to them: 'The harvest is rich but the workers are few; therefore ask the harvest-master to send workers to his harvest' " (Lk. 10:1-2). The seventy-two returned to the Lord Jesus and were very excited and jubilant when they realized the tremendous powers that the Lord had given them: "Master, even the demons are subject to us in your name" (Lk. 10:17). Then Jesus told them to be more jubilant in the fact that their names are inscribed in heaven: "At that moment Jesus rejoiced in the Holy Spirit and said: 'I offer you praise, O Father, Lord of heaven and earth, because what you have hidden from the learned and the clever you have revealed to the merest children. Yes, Father, you have graciously willed it so. Everything has been given over to me by my Father. No one knows the Son except the Father and no one knows the Father except the Son—and anyone to whom the Son wishes to reveal him' " (Lk. 10:21-22).

Today it is the same Lord Jesus alive and living in his body. There is much more to being a parishioner than attending church and perhaps belonging to some society. There awaits us an experience of community when we learn to become a people.

The pastor and associates of a parish are much more than custodians of parish buildings. The pastor is true shepherd, as the Lord is shepherd; he is a convener of charisms. He it is who must call forth the gifts in the body. He it is who must tenderly nurture these gifts of the Spirit in those he serves. It will never happen until he stands in the midst of the people and joins with them in prayer to the Father that his Son may be brought to birth in the hearts of the people.

"I pray also for those who will believe in me through their word, that all may be one, as you, Father, are in me, and I in you; I pray that they may be one in us, that the world may believe that you sent me" (Jn. 17:18-21).

Is not a pastor like the Lord Jesus in his parish when he joins with his people in prayer, discerning the Father's will for his people, recognizing the gifts and charisms in the body and sending forth his brothers and sisters to serve each other?

In our time we call people pastoral ministers. Are they not modern disciples? Are the powers the Lord gave to those he sent forward to be denied to the modern minister? I believe not. I believe that these same gifts are in his body today. We are beginning to realize them and see ourselves more as a people alive in the Lord.

A parish alive to the Lord's presence will be open to using all the most modern techniques of selectivity, management, and supervision at its disposal. The Lord wants us to use the methods and systems that we have for effective ministry in our modern world. We will therefore consider the formation of our pastoral care team in the light of modern techniques as applied to parish structures as they exist presently. They will develop, grow, and perhaps change to the degree that we are open to the promptings of his Spirit living within his body.

5
Selection, Management and Supervision

A pastor is a convener of charisms. He should invite the entire Christian community to a role of service. Every member should know that he is welcome to step forward. The concept of lay-ministry should be presented to everyone in the community. The Lord will send forth the workers to gather the harvest if we pray the Lord of the harvest. Some parishes use the pulpit exclusively to sensitize people to the needs around them. Some parishes use their monthly or weekly bulletins to back up the talks from the pulpit. How people are given the invitation will differ in each parish and area.

It would be a beautiful sight if the priests, religious and laity met in a body once a week outside of Sunday worship to pray together to discern the Lord's plan for that parish. What a power would be released in that parish! Ministries would evolve, people would get to truly know each other, people would be served, Jesus' body would grow, and the parish would come alive in the Lord. In this way persons could be selected on the basis of their talents and gifts. People who would not be "as gifted" as others would be assigned tasks where their gifts could find expression. I know a retarded girl who visits people in a home for adults. She is pleasant and brings many hours of companionship to some people who have taken an interest in her and are teaching her sewing skills. This is a visible example of the Lord serving those who step forward to serve.

From those who come forward, people will be chosen and selected for specific ministries on the basis of availability, commitment, special gifts, dependability, ability to serve as part of a team, sociability, friendliness, openness, spirituality, creativity, and self-actualizing.

Selection will occur after a group begins to realize itself as a people. People will begin to experience each other in prayer. Gifts, talents, and charisms will emerge as those in the group develop interpersonal relationships. Ministries will emerge as a result of need and because someone present in the body has the gifts or charism to fulfill that need.

Some people may wish to come into the group to support the group in prayer. They presently do not have time to serve a special need because they are meeting personal needs or family needs or for other reasons of a personal nature. Perhaps, in the future, these circumstances will change. Do not exclude such persons. In fact, many times people have to discontinue temporarily a ministry they are engaged in for personal reasons. People ought to feel free to do this and yet continue to come together in the body for prayer.

Someone with the gift or charism of organizing and managing should be selected to be the manager of the body. Much of the organization of the organism will depend on this person's gifts. The Lord will use him or her to supply leadership to the body. Managing the team may not need the gifts of a pastor or even need his power of orders. Management and leadership in this area may sometimes best be served by a qualified religious or lay person. The person chosen for this position should possess leadership qualities and managerial skills.

Many parishes have hired full-time salaried persons such as religious sisters or brothers. Sometimes a retired person serves as manager. However, it is important that this person have the time and energy for this position. Whether or not this person receives some recompense for his work is up to the parish. Some retired persons would welcome the added income, especially if they themselves live on a fixed income.

Some parishes function very well with a volunteer manager. But if his time is limited, a growing body which generates more involved needs can become a very formidable task for a volunteer.

Supervision and consultation are very important for the proper and effective functioning of the body. The human body from time to time must have regular checkups. We need to consult a professional—a doctor —to see if we are functioning well. In the same way the body of the Lord needs to be supervised. This process is carried out in the Lord's body through a system of self-evaluation, back-up consultation and supervision.

In evaluating itself, the group will take a look at what is happening within the group in prayer and among themselves to see what they are becoming. They will take a look at the tasks they are doing in terms of meeting the needs of those being served. Every community must have within itself professional support for a group such as this. It should have social workers who can be consulted, nurses, doctors, community groups, and societies which are eager to help. They become the persons and groups that the manager can consult for assistance with special problems. If some of these persons become part of the body, they serve in ministry in a supervisory capacity by helping in case review, placement, teaching basic nursing skills and the like.

A manager should learn the resources present in his or her immediate community. The parish church need not feel that it has to duplicate services already being provided in a community. In a large city, the manager will find a full range of resources upon which he can call for help.

A hospital in the area can be invaluable to a manager for professional advice and back-up services. The manager should get to know the administrator of the hospital, social service personnel, nurses and doctors who are willing to help a community prevent problems, and to help in their resolution when they occur.

Pastoral care includes much more than sacramental ministry and extraordinary ministry of the Eucharist. Jesus met the hunger needs of the multitude before he taught them. Many times it is these very human needs that must be satisfied first.

I dream of a diocese alive in the Lord Jesus. I envision a revolution in a parish free enough to call itself forth from the tomb of ritualism, apathy, formal structures and prejudices.

Teenagers may minister by systematically combing the neighborhood to find those in need. Properly identified with the parish, and working in teams, they could bring back to the body information about the homebound. A religious sister hired to manage the team could follow up the leads, make contact with the person, note some of the person's needs and bring information back to the body.

Ministries will evolve as each need is recognized and identified. The needs will vary with the make-up of the parish, with social, ethnic and cultural differences.

Ministers will find problems which touch on basic

living, such as the need for a homemaker, poverty of life, and financial needs which come from trying to live on a fixed income, and meeting the rising costs of housing, food, medicines. Problems of trying to find meaningful employment, health care, nutrition, decent housing, companionship, and fear of the streets will be found as realities in the experience of those whose lives are touched.

I dream of a Christian community rising to itself as a people of God, Spirit-filled and alive with the love of the Lord Jesus. Pastoral ministers will come forward, ordinary people, Spirit-filled and willing to wash the feet of their brothers and sisters. Such ministries are evolving now in communities. Among them are telephone reassurance services, friendly visitors, transportation aides, companions who take people to the doctor, shopping centers, the park, or a lending library, bringing the homebound to church on Sunday, bringing the elderly from nursing homes and residences to church with the family, inviting the lonely to share family occasionally, eucharistic ministers ministering to the homebound and shut-ins, including nursing homes and hospitals, helping with the special problems that the elderly have because of failing sight, hearing, and other handicaps, medicare and medicaid information, social security problems, and special problems of handicapped persons and mentally retarded.

Each parish or area (some parishes are joining together to meet special needs in an area) will develop differently but with a unity where Jesus is truly the Lord and he serves his body through each of us.

Someday this will be a living reality around the world. It may be a dream, but the Spirit is making it a reality. I know. I see it happening.

6
Face-to-Face Encounter

When Christians meet, they create a body—the living Jesus among us. Each of us has the presence of the living God within us. We are made in his image and likeness, but we become his image and likeness only when the core of our beings are touched with the life of God living within us in such a manner that we ourselves magnify and mirror the living God. The more this process takes place, the more we are transformed into the likeness of the Son, and we become more our true and real selves.

The coming together, the meeting, is the vehicle in which this process has its impetus. Brothers and sisters in the Lord come together in meetings to pray, share information, discern needs, make recommendations, assign tasks, go forth to minister (do the tasks), and report back to the body at the next meeting to pray, share information, discern needs, make recommendations, assign tasks, go forth to minister (do the tasks), and report back to the body at the next meeting. And so the process continues and the body is nurtured and grows.

The conduct of the body is a face-to-face encounter with each other. Each member should make a point to get to know all the members by name. Time should be provided before and after each meeting so that members will have an opportunity to encounter each other. At other times a day of recollection with free time would be a great help, or a parish picnic or a get-together at the park or beach. One parish meets twice a month. One week they meet to pray and socialize. Another week they meet to pray briefly and conduct a business meeting.

I would consider a knowledge of each person in the body a priority for the group. The manager of the body acts as the center. He convenes the body, calling the members together to pray. He leads the meeting and calls for the sharing of the information, inviting each one to share in turn. After all the information is expressed to the entire body, the members are invited to make recommendations about the information and discern specific needs. The manager will identify the needs expressed and set priorities. He will then assign the tasks, and the ministers will go forth to carry out their ministries.

Organization is vitally important initially and will become increasingly important as the body grows, develops and more needs are discerned and included.

The usual functioning of an organization is that decisions are made from the top down with the head or leader making all the decisions and the members carrying out the tasks. What is being suggested here is that the group share in all the processes of praying, gathering information, making recommendations, assigning tasks (ministries), and reporting back. The manager is not a "boss." He does not make all the decisions. He shares in the decision-making process.

The team approach to pastoral ministries must be conceived as a wheel. The manager is the axis around which the spokes revolve, each spoke being initially important, necessary and a contributing factor to the strength and vitality of the total wheel. The outer rim which encircles the wheel represents those being served. The center is the love of Jesus which binds them all together.

The Meeting—A Summary

All meetings should begin in the awareness that those present have gathered as the body of Lord Jesus to discern the Father's plan for this body. All should be very open to the Spirit guiding the process through the discussions, discernment and decisions.

All meetings should be conducted in the atmosphere of sharing and decision-making on the part of the entire group.

The following is a manner of conducting meetings which may prove helpful.

The manager, after about fifteen minutes of shared prayer, identifies what is to be discussed and leads the formal discussions.

1. *Share Information:* A target (need) is presented. All members with information about the target should share it with the entire group. All information should relate to the target. Private conversation should be discouraged—it is a sign someone is not interested in what is being discussed. After all the information is shared, move on to making recommendations.

2. *Making Recommendations:* Urge all the members to share what they think ought to be done about the specific target (need). Listen to everyone who makes a recommendation (suggestion as how the need can be met). Recommendations should be specific. "Somebody ought to . . ." should be removed from our vocabulary. List the recommendations, go over them with the group, and get a consensus of opinion as to a course of action. Sometimes the course of action recommended is to go out again and get more informa-

tion. This then would become an identifiable task. Sometimes a concrete recommendation is agreed upon. Then that concrete recommendation becomes an identifiable task.

3. *Identify Tasks:* Once the target (need) is identified, a task is formulated from the recommendations. The target (need): Who are the shut-ins in our parish? The recommendation: Concentrate on a specific block in the parish. Organize a group of six people, going two by two, to canvas the block for frail elderly, sick, handicapped, or isolated persons. Have I.D. cards for people. Ask help from the police department. People may be afraid to open doors. Identify task: specific people are to begin the project of finding the forgotten. Report back. When identifying a task, it should be specific with specific goals. The group should agree upon the task and its priority.

4. *Assignment of Tasks:* The manager selects the person or persons to carry out the task to minister. The task may be relatively on-going, such as visiting a hospital or nursing home or bringing Communion to the home-bound or visiting a shut-in. It may be temporary, like the placement of a frail elderly person, or a ride to the doctor. If a group of persons is involved in a specific ministry, one of the group should be selected by the manager as the person-in-charge. That person is responsible for reporting back to the body, but anyone in the group is free to add to the report. All reports are made verbally to the group and a written outline of the report is given to the manager.

5. *Evaluating the Tasks:* The immediate evaluation of the task is done by the group after the report is made. The task is discussed to see if the goal was accomplished and if any further recommendations should be made. This process gives support to all concerned. It

helps the group to realize that all should be concerned, not just the particular ministers. It helps the body to expand its vision and grow in its awareness of those serving and being served. This is the dynamic of the living Jesus.

6. *Next Meeting:* Set the time, date and place for the next meeting. Anyone not present should take the initiative in finding out what went on and when the next meeting will be held. Many times a specific day or days each month are designated. The meeting is vitally important to the growth of the body. The meetings should be concerned with the people being served. The ministers should be encouraged at a point in the meetings to share their experiences with ministry to particular persons. They should be encouraged to share experiences which will be of benefit to all. Failures should be shared. After all, not everyone accepted Jesus. Should we expect one hundred percent success?

A typical meeting may be conducted in the following manner. The pastoral ministers gather together about a half-hour before the meeting begins. This enables the ministers to get to know each other. Sometimes coffee is provided, and it is also available throughout the meeting.

After a time, the manager calls the meeting together. At least fifteen minutes should be devoted to prayer. During this time of prayer the Lord should be asked to send his Spirit upon the ministers so that they may become one. Prayer for specific people to whom they are ministering may be mentioned. Prayer for those serving, for persons still unknown, for needs not discerned, and for the building of his Kingdom is in order. Prayer for specific persons or friends of the ministers is in order. Prayer of praise to the Lord, asking his anointing upon his ministers and those they serve, is in order. Whatever form of prayer the ministers choose is fine. The important thing is that they pray together and not that someone "says a prayer."

After praying together, the manager introduces information on a specific topic, need, program, or whatever has to be discussed. He permits everyone who so wishes to add information. What to do about it will come after all the information about a target is known. A target is whatever the body wishes to discuss. It is the object of the information.

Once all the information is known, then the manager moves the group on to making recommendations about the information. It may well be that no recommendations to resolve the problem can be made due to a lack of information. Then the recommendation would be to get more information for the next meeting.

If there is enough information to make specific recommendations, they are made by any of the ministers; they are discussed, and a specific recommendation or recommendations are decided upon.

In line with the recommendation a task is formulated and assigned to one of the ministers. It may be a permanent task agreed upon or a temporary task which may last until the next meeting when it is reported upon.

This method may be used for each item (target). It is only one method of conducting a meeting but it will prove helpful in the group, being very specific about what it does.

The manager should repeat the tasks decided upon and those persons selected to carry them out.

A time should be set for the next meeting unless a definite schedule of meetings is already agreed upon.

The ministers may be encouraged to share experiences in their ministry at this point. The meeting may be brought to a close with a Scripture reading or another reading which may have touched someone during the past week.

Time should also be set aside for socializing. This is very important. The pastoral ministers must have time together to get to know each other and enjoy each other's company in the process of becoming a body.

By way of example here is how one group of pastoral ministers took an item (target) and brought it through the meeting. This parish had as part of its ministry the visitation of a nursing home. After the pastoral ministers were visiting the nursing home for a period of months, problems arose with some of the residents who began to make demands upon the pastoral ministers.

One problem was brought up at a meeting by a pastoral minister: "One woman has been asking me for money and has been getting angry with me when I refuse. She also is demanding that I visit her three times a week. Nothing I do seems to satisfy her." With this statement of fact other ministers began to bring up similar requests on the part of the residents. It seemed that the pastoral minister was not alone in this problem. Other residents were asking for gifts, newspapers, and special favors. All ministers were asked to share similar experiences. As a result, a target was formulated by the manager. "Residents asking for money, newspapers, gifts, special favors."

The manager then opened the meeting up to the group for making recommendations about the target: "What can we do about it?" Someone suggested that our ministry should be limited only to prayer and friendly visiting. Someone else suggested that we visit only once a week. Another suggestion was to start a fund in the group for specific needs of the residents. Still another pastoral minister suggested that the manager speak with the administrator of the home. A further suggestion was to speak with the social service office.

A discussion began about the recommendations. Each suggestion was considered. Someone suggested that we invite the head of the social service office to join the group on a regular basis, so that when they discussed the residents and their problems she would be able to give professional input.

The task formulated was to approach the head of the social service office with this suggestion. The manager was given the task and was to report back to the group at the next meeting.

The person contacted was delighted with the request and the interest of the group. She has been invaluable and has also been a tremendous source of professional help and back-up to the group of pastoral ministers who serve the home-bound. She has been able to make suggestions concerning placement, food stamps, medicaid, and medicare as well as many insights into helping the elderly with their problems.

7
Educating and
Training the Body

The Lord gives each of us a gift or charism to be
used in the service of others. The gift is something given
to each one for the sole purpose of being given away.
Yet how the gift is used is very much influenced by the
human knowledge we add to ourselves through education and training. Someone may have a gift in management. We call him or her a "born leader." But how
much better this person manages when he has studied
management and systems. Someone may enter social
work because he has a special gift in helping people
with some very basic human needs. How much more effective will be his work if he has studied social work.

The pastoral minister will certainly be a far more
effective instrument in his ministry and a greater
witness to the Lord if he is educated and trained.

Education and training must be planned and organized. The intensity, degree and level of education
and training will depend upon the minister, the ministry
and the needs of the person who is ministered to. Depending upon the extent to which a person wishes to
minister will he enter into levels of education and training. For example, a pastoral minister who would find
his ministry to be service to patients in a dialysis unit or

coronary care unit of a hospital would need a different level of training than the pastoral minister assisting at Mass in the parish church or the pastoral minister who would visit a shut-in and bring the Eucharist.

Levels of education and training should be provided to the pastoral ministers. The content and training should be tailored to meet the minister's needs as he grows in ministry.

However, there are some basic levels of education and training that are simple to plan and organize. The first level would be a basic knowledge of pastoral care; the second level would be built upon this knowledge and include pastoral counseling; the third level would specialize in ministry to patients in specialized hospital units—emergency room ministry, special ministry to the terminally ill, elderly and handicapped. Naturally, each of these levels will admit of degree and intensity depending upon the needs of a diocese, an area or a parish.

In developing a level it ought to include both the didactic and the clinical. It will be necessary to provide classroom teaching, lectures, workshops, and seminars as well as the practical application of this learning with "in-service" training under supervision.

I would suggest that the first level include such topics as:

1. a theology of pastoral care;
2. a theology of sickness;
3. practical aspects of visiting the sick;
4. psychological attitudes that accompany sickness;
5. ministering to terminal patients;
6. the aging process and problems of the elderly person;
7. ministering to the elderly;

8. needs of physically and mentally handicapped persons;

9. ministering to the handicapped;

10. the sacraments of the Eucharist, reconciliation, and anointing of the sick, and ministering to people by leading them to the touch of the Lord;

11. practical aspects of celebrating the sacraments;

12. prayer and how to pray with people.

If there is a hospital, nursing home or residence in the community, those who would serve by visiting and ministering in these institutions should receive training on the floors with the patients and under a supervisor. It is worth the time and effort for the priest to teach pastoral ministers how to visit the sick, elderly or handicapped, assuming that the priest knows himself. I have found hospital personnel extremely helpful in this area. The best teachers are those who combine knowledge with a heart.

After the pastoral minister has served his brothers and sisters in ministry for a period of time and has had some experience, a second level of education and training could be offered. The pastor or the manager may wish to select specific pastoral ministers who have the time and aptitude to receive further training. This training should include a basic psychology of human development and growth, study of mental disorders, principles of pastoral counseling, and practical experience in counseling under supervision. A number of people trained in this way can be invaluable to a parish. Many religious have been trained in pastoral counseling and may wish to volunteer as teachers. Psychiatric social workers or psychiatric nurses are other potential sources as teachers. Psychologists and psychiatrists sometimes are very willing to help train pastoral ministers to recognize problems in people that may need professional help. A psychiatric hospital may be willing to offer courses for ministers, priests, rabbis and pastoral ministers which would help the community.

A basic course for the pastoral ministers in social work and case work could easily be scheduled. If the diocese has a Catholic Charities agency, this would be a resource for such a course.

A third level of education should be specialization. The blind, the deaf, the mentally retarded, the physically handicapped need pastoral ministers who are knowledgeable and have received some special training.

The parish should look to the diocese or the community for agencies or associations who are usually only too willing to help train people in these specialities. Again, a parish should be aware of the resources in the local area. They are usually there. We need only to tap into them.

Any priest who has served as a chaplain to a hospital has felt the frustration of not being able to minister to all those who use the facility for medical treatment. There are areas of the hospital where pastoral ministers are so needed. The clinics, the emergency room, the coronary care unit, the intensive care unit, in fact all the special units of the hospital, are places where trained ministers can truly help their brothers and sisters. Patients with special needs, those with terminal diseases, their families, and amputees are among the people who need time, concern and help from trained pastoral ministers. But what about the remainder of the patients—possibly the bulk of the patients—who are not in special units? They need care too, and very often a solitary chaplain is unable to give it. The one priest-one hospital concept of chaplaincy is no longer valid or authentic. Pastoral care involves much more than one priest can possibly give. The priest of the future will have to work as part of a team of trained pastoral ministers.

The administration, nurses, and resident doctors will welcome the trained pastoral minister. Many times they are all too willing to share in his or her training. The pastor or his associate should be part of the training and offer whatever support he can in developing this area of ministry.

These three levels of education and training are by no means exhaustive in what the pastoral ministers can and should learn. They should be urged to avail themselves of programs, workshops and seminars which will give them greater expertise in helping others.

This degree of education and training can be planned and organized by a local parish. With the suggestions made above, a parish can easily begin to educate and train its own pastoral ministers within a community. A community has many resources within itself which if utilized can be of tremendous help. We should not feel that we must have all the resources contained within the Church. We should look to the secular community and our brothers and sisters of other faiths to join in whatever efforts are common to us all.

The education and training of team managers are essential to order and effectiveness. Most times we do not bother with giving special training to the person who will manage the pastoral ministers. This person should be given particular consideration and attention. I would suggest that if he has not had management training, then he should receive it.

There should be a complete understanding and communication between the pastor and the manager. He should know his role in the body. In presenting the program, its publicity, its integration into the life of the parish, and its relationship to the parish council and the other parish societies should be discussed and be clear to everyone. I would recommend that the manager be a member of the parish council by reason of his position.

What I have suggested by way of education and training for the pastoral ministers and the manager is basic to a community of believers beginning to involve itself in reaching out to their brothers and sisters in need. The time and effort involved in this area will return a hundred-fold as pastoral ministers enter into ministry with knowledge and competence.

8
Supervision and Professional Back-up

After the Lord had sent out the seventy-two they returned to him to tell him all that had happened. The supervision suggested here is more or less in the same dynamic.

The pastoral ministers come together and share problems, difficulties, successes, and failures. This is a process of supervision and evaluation. The pastoral ministers evaluate themselves in terms of meeting the specific needs they previously identified. From time to time professional people may be invited to help in supervising and evaluating and as a source for consultation. At times social workers can monitor cases and help review cases with ministers, making suggestions as to procedure and disposition.

Other professionals may be invited into the group to share their expertise on a particular problem confronting the ministers. Perhaps a particular team is ministering at a nursing home where there are an exceptional number of alcoholics. Having someone with expertise in this area to help monitor the ministry by being at the meetings when particular people are discussed would be invaluable.

From time to time the body must evaluate itself in

the light of its purpose and be open to the truth that this is the Lord's body and he is its power and strength and head.

Professional back-up to the body is a must. The parish itself may have professionals willing to minister to the ministers in the capacity of supervision, evaluation of cases and consultation. A parish should know all its community resources. It should know the persons involved in centers or institutions who can be relied on for consultation and referral.

I would suggest that a community be familiar with such resources as the local hospital can offer. Every hospital has a component of services which attempts to meet the needs of the consumers from the community who use the hospital. Most hospitals have a social service department, a volunteer department, and a community relations department. Besides the usual departments found in every hospital these three departments can be invaluable to the local community as a help with professional back-up assistance.

The directors of these hospitals are usually only too willing to help local groups to develop reach-out programs. Many times the director or a representative will lecture to the group or invite the group to the hospital for lectures and orientation. Sometimes, if a good rapport exists with the local parish, a case worker will help by reviewing cases once a week which are uncovered by the pastoral ministers and are in need of social assistance. They can make tremendous suggestions as to contacts to make and where to go for assistance.

Some volunteer departments conduct courses for community people in first aid, homemaking and practical nursing. When pastoral ministers serve a hospital, a nursing home or an institution where there is a volunteer department, they should become part of the department and then be assigned to pastoral care. It is an excellent idea even from a protection point of view. The pastoral minister would be assured of being covered by insurance if he were hurt while serving at the hospital and receive benefits which are many times given to volunteers by way of a service and in appreciation for services rendered to the patients. These benefits sometimes include a complete physical examination yearly, free meals and invitations to important events celebrated by the institution. The pastoral minister gives a service that is recognized as an integral part of the healing process. He should consider his ministry as essential to the hospital.

The community relations department of a hospital is an extremely valuable resource. Community relations people usually know all the pertinent and relevant resources in a community and what each agency or organization provides by way of services. They can also be of tremendous help in acquainting the local group with all the resources that are present in the hospital.

Many communities have agencies willing to help with problems of child abuse, adoption, elderly persons, alcoholism, the blind, hard of hearing, physically handicapped, mentally retarded, medicaid, medicare, and social security. The agencies and services will depend upon the size of the community. There are a great many services available if we take the time to investigate. To a reach-out group they can be invaluable for the training of the groups, for supervision, or for consultation.

The investigation of these resources can easily be one of the first tasks that the pastoral care team should undertake. Personal visits should be made by members of the group, particularly those members who will be contacting these persons for assistance. This will help to develop a personal approach to all those persons in a neighborhood who are involved in delivering services to those in need.

Through this first step a people could become a neighborhood and grow into a community.

9
Ministry to the Homebound and Shut-Ins

It is always a concern on the part of pastoral ministers just beginning in ministry as to how to approach some person in the parish whom they don't know. "I don't have a Roman collar. It's easy for you. You are recognized. They will let you in. People look for you. Maybe they won't want to receive Holy Communion from me. People want the priest to come. What will I say? What if they want to receive the sacrament of reconciliation?" These are statements and concerns of many pastoral ministers I have met. They are common concerns but arise more from the fears of the pastoral minister than from the person behind the locked door.

The person behind the curtain, in bed for years, alone and unable to go out, undernourished, sick, elderly, handicapped, lonely, hungry, depressed, anxious, fearful, blind, hard of hearing, or whatever his human condition, is not concerned with what you will say as long as you speak, with what you look like as long as you come, with what you wear as long as you care, with who you are as long as you bring the Lord Jesus, with

50

all your credentials as long as you can help him in his need.

It is a real concern that whoever comes to the door is a friendly face and not that of a fellow human bent on doing him harm. Fear of violence is a reality in our society and one about which the Church and pastoral ministers must be keenly aware. Persons must be reassured that the person knocking on that door or ringing that doorbell is truly a pastoral minister and not someone else. This is a priority that should not be overlooked or taken lightly. In very dangerous neighborhoods a preliminary visit by a priest or a sister, possibly involving the help of the local police precinct or recognizable community people, would be in order.

When we speak of a shut-in, most people think of a very elderly person, living alone and sick. This description would fit many parishioners who are truly shut-ins. But when I speak of a shut-in, I am also referring to people of all ages—teenagers afflicted with cystic fibrosis, cancer, or paralyzed; young adults crippled with multiple sclerosis; spastics; middle-aged persons with a variety of disabilities carried over from youth; young elderly with severe heart disorders. Shut-ins can mean anyone. Shut-ins come in all sizes, shapes, sexes and ages. All shut-ins are people. It is not we and they. It is "we," and one of us is a shut-in. I must reach out and care.

Our approach and attitude will be influenced by how we think about people when we visit them. If we approach people with the attitude that they are somehow different because they are sick, elderly or handicapped, then our pastoral approach will convey this attitude. We must learn to look beyond the problem and see a human being with all the same feelings that we have.

There was a young girl, seven years of age, dying of leukemia at a hospital where I once served as a chaplain. She was a beautiful little girl. Her name was Lauria. She influenced my life very much. It was my privilege to celebrate with her her First Holy Communion and to celebrate the sacrament of confirmation with her. I feel that the Lord gave her knowledge far beyond her years.

She spoke to me freely about God and that she was going home to be with him. This was the faith that her parents had given her. Her one true concern was for her father. She felt that he would find her dying a terrible loss. She asked me to see that he did not hurt too badly. She knew that he would miss her very much. I lived through her death with her for a period of eight months. I see her as vividly now as I did then—her beautiful long golden hair braided on top of her head, and her wide blue and so very wise eyes that seemed to say "It's all right; I really don't mind dying." She didn't just know about God; she experienced his presence. When we talked, there was a peace and joy in her voice when she spoke about Jesus. I was able to share this with her family after she died.

Her father did take her sickness and eventual death very hard. I visited with the family for nearly a year afterward. The Lord had used Lauria's mother and father to bring a deep faith to her. He used Lauria to bring his presence to the family. Her older brother Anthony, who was twelve, told me after her death that he was not sad at all. She used to talk with him about going home. She truly believed that God was waiting for her.

Our ministry should, above all else, be human. God became one of us in order to show us that it is through our humanity that he saves us. We must be, at all times, sensitive to people's feelings. There is nothing wrong in feelings. They are human. I remembered a young man who ripped a medal of the Sacred Heart from his neck and threw it at me. "Take your God," he shouted at me. "He let my father die!" I picked up his medal, put it in his pocket and said to him: "I can understand your feeling that way—you must be hurting terribly." He was a fellow human being deeply hurt. I don't think God minded at all. Why should I?

We may find ourselves visiting a person who is bedridden. It would be wise to take a little time before visiting to pray for the person and try to understand what it must be like to never get out of bed, and to have people taking care of your every need. Elizabeth is seventy-two years old. She is a widow. Her three daughters are her family. One of her daughters has become a eucharistic minister and brings the Eucharist to her mother every day. Her mother had attended daily Mass at the parish church for the past fifty years. The pastoral practice of bringing Holy Communion only on First Fridays or once a month should be abolished. Anyone wishing to receive the Eucharist daily should have the opportunity. We must reach out.

For those pastoral ministers who find visiting home-bound or shut-ins uncomfortable, perhaps these few suggestions would help to make your visit enjoyable and relaxed, not to say rewarding.

You are being sent to this person, at this time and in this place. You are the visible Jesus. He wants to use you—not another minister, but you. Pray for the person before you visit. Ask the Lord Jesus to use you in whatever way he wishes. Ask him to put in your mind and in your heart exactly what he wants you to say, and how he wants you to say it.

If you are bringing the Eucharist, then ask Jesus to take you. Remember, it is Jesus who saves, but he does it through you; it is Jesus who comforts through you; it is Jesus who touches hearts through you. You are the most important person who will visit that person today.

Your coming together with that person in the name of Jesus makes him present to the situation—truly present. So, why be fearful or anxious. Trust him. He needs you.

Be yourself when you visit, and especially when you are bringing the Eucharist. Don't become "churchy." Greet the person. Take a few minutes to inquire how the person is. See that there is water present or at least know where to get it. Share the homily with the person if you are going forth from Mass. Take time to pray with the person. Celebrate Jesus in the sacrament. Don't just distribute Communion. If there are other persons present, invite them to share the Eucharist if they so wish. Bring enough hosts so that you will not have to break them. You can always return to the tabernacle. Wait reverently until the person has swallowed. Share a final prayer and bless the person with the pyx if the Eucharist is still remaining.

If your visit does not include the Eucharist, be open to sharing a cup of tea or coffee with the person. Let handicapped people serve you in their homes even if you have the urge to do it for them. Remember, you are the visitor.

None of us has a right to enter into another person's life unless we are invited. We have a tendency to push our way into people's lives, especially when they are sick, elderly or handicapped. Respect people's rights. But if you are invited to share another's life, be open to a tremendously rewarding experience. There is a beauty in every human being which can only be re-alized when we get close enough and take the time to be truly human. This experience of another is a gift. Cherish it.

10
Ministry to the Hospitalized, Some Specialties— Some Handicaps

The sick—how Jesus loved them. "Jesus summoned the twelve and began to send them out two by two, giving them authority over unclean spirits. He instructed them to take nothing on the journey but a walking stick—no food, no traveling bag, not a coin in the purses in their belts. . . . With that they went off, preaching the need of repentance. They expelled many demons, anointed the sick with oil, and worked many cures" (Mk. 6:7-8, 12-13).

"After making the crossing they came ashore at Gennesaret, and tied up there. As they were leaving the boat people immediately recognized him. The crowds scurried about the adjacent area and began to bring in the sick on bedrolls to the place where they heard he was. Wherever he put in an appearance, in villages, in towns, or at crossroads, they laid the sick in the market places and begged him to let them touch just the tassel of his cloak. All who touched him got well" (Mk. 6:53-56).

Shouldn't our faith tell us that Jesus is with us as we minister to our brothers and sisters who are sick? Should we not be encouraged knowing that Jesus is with us as we walk the corridors of a modern hospital?

Should we not step out in faith knowing that our brother and Savior Jesus is the healer? The power of the Father's love is flowing through the body of his Son today.

So often we fear to go to sick people, not knowing what to say or how to help. "I wouldn't know what to say to someone who had cancer." "What do you say to a person whom you don't even know?" "What if the person doesn't want visitors?" "People know who you are—you're the priest. They want to see you." "I would be scared to death to visit a hospital." "Is it hard to learn how to do it?" "I think I would faint if someone told me that he was going to have his leg amputated." "With all those machines and tubes and things, I wouldn't be able to."

I have heard these same remarks over and over from ordinary people who turned out to be anything but ordinary. Most people experience some such feelings, especially if they are not familiar with hospitals. Most people never brush shoulders with the medical profession except when the reason is personal. Perhaps a loved one was in the hospital, or perhaps they at one time were patients themselves.

One woman told me that she stood outside the first room she was to visit for nearly three minutes before entering. She was frightened at the prospect of visiting two total strangers. I asked her how she handled her fear, because today she is a fantastic minister, touching people in ways that can only be inspired by the Lord. She told me, "Father, I thought to myself that if I don't walk into that room, then Jesus will never get there. He only has my feet at this moment. So I walked in. It was beautiful. There was a young man about twenty-five in the room who was about to undergo surgery for a tumor on his parotid gland. At the time, I had no idea where the parotid gland was. It could have been anywhere. He pointed to a gland behind his ear. I gave him Holy Communion and prayed with him for his operation and asked the Lord to heal him. He held my hand and prayed with me. When I left that room, I just knew that I belonged." This woman has been a pastoral minister for two years.

The pastoral minister to the institutionalized sick must be aware of his or her mission as an official member of the body sent forth to bring the total concern and care of the body to the member who is sick. He bears the good news that Jesus is alive, that he cares, that he is concerned, that he loves us and extends his hand to each of us when we are in need. Jesus is alive in his body. He is the head and we are his members. Jesus is sick, dying of cancer, frightened, alone, worrying about an operation, concerned about his family.

The pastoral minister brings the same compassion, the same care and the same love that Jesus showed to those who pressed forward to touch the hem of his garment, to experience the power flowing from him. He is Jesus walking the corridors of the hospital serving the suffering members of his body. We are members of Jesus' body, and it is through the pastoral minister that the body of Jesus is served. He is the feet of Jesus walking into a hospital room. He is the hands of Jesus extended in friendliness. He is the eyes of Jesus looking compassionately on the suffering. He is the ears of Jesus listening to his suffering brothers and offering consoling words. He is the heart of Jesus filled with concern, love and compassion, entering into the very life of his suffering brothers and sharing with him the common bond of mortality. He can understand his brother being fearful and frightened, uneasy, anxious and embarrassed because he shares these same feelings. The pastoral minister brings Jesus to his brother in the

person of himself in order that he may share himself
with his brother who is in need. It is his brother's need
that is most important, and it is in responding to this
need that the pastoral minister fulfills his ministry.
Jesus is alive today serving his brother through the living out of his presence in the pastoral minister.

It is the warmth and affection of the loving Jesus
that are given birth to when the pastoral minister enters
the room of his suffering brother. He may be bringing
him Jesus in the Eucharist or making the Lord present
as he comes together in prayer with his suffering
brother. The same Jesus who walked our world and
stretched out his hand to the sick and spoke the words
of consolation and touched his suffering brother with
the power of his healing is made present in the
sickroom. Jesus has come.

Just as the Lord sent his apostles to minister two
by two, so today we are learning to share ministry as
teams. Each member of the team has the support of the
other. Many parishes are organizing parish pastoral
care teams to respond to the institutionalized and
home-bound sick in their parishes. Most times the pastor has hired a full-time pastoral person, usually a religious sister, to manage the program. This person could
also be a deacon, a religious brother or lay person. The
manager in many situations acts as the chaplain to the
hospital. During the visitation the manager and the pastoral ministers prepare a list of patients to be seen by
the priest. This list indicates the room and bed number
and reason for the request.

Pastors of parishes ministering to hospitals should
provide some very basic pastoral ministry on a daily
basis. This should include visitation of new admissions
to the hospital from the previous day, pre-ops (those
undergoing surgery the following day), and all critically

ill patients. Provision for the daily reception of Holy
Communion should be made. Provision for emergency
calls should always be made.

Many parishes have begun a ministry of visitation
to all the patients at the hospital. Through the ministry
of a pastoral care team, priests, religious and laity may
visit the hospital. After the administration of the hospital has been consulted concerning the program, the
team members should meet with the administrator and
other staff such as the directors of nursing, social service, medicine and surgery.

Perhaps these suggestions will help the team to organize its visit to the hospital.

If the team meets at the hospital, one person
should bring the Eucharist from the church. The team
should meet in a specified room, perhaps the nurses'
lounge or the volunteer office. This meeting should be
worked out with the administration so that the room is
available. The manager should go over the list, made
the previous week, of patients for whom they have
prayed during the week. The Eucharist is distributed to
each member of the team for his or her pyx. Prayer
should be offered together for the people they are about
to meet. The Lord should be asked to use the members
of the team in whatever way he wishes and to direct
them to whomever he wishes to touch.

The team members then go to their assigned
floors. The floor should be visited by beginning at both
ends of the floor and working toward the center. Each
room and bed should be visited. The number of ministers assigned to each floor will depend upon the number
of patients. All patients should be visited, not just Catholics.

On each floor the team members should stop at
the nurses' station. They should let the nurse know that

they are on the floor and report back when they are leaving the floor. The head nurse should be asked if anyone has made any specific requests—if there is a particular patient who may need special help or if there are patients who may need the sacrament of anointing. The priest or manager of the team should visit the head nursing office to check on specific people who need to be visited.

The pastoral visit should be personal. The minister should introduce himself by name. He should say that he is part of a Catholic pastoral care team from the local parish. Mentioning the name of the priest involved is an excellent idea, for in that way the team is identified with the clergy. The religious affiliation of the patient can be determined by asking: "What church do you attend?" Do not ask, "Are you Catholic?" If the person is not Catholic, ask what particular denomination the person belongs to, and then carry on from there. There is no reason not to ask the person if he or she may wish the minister to pray with him or her.

When the patient is Catholic, the minister should tell the person that he is a special minister to bring Holy Communion and that he has the Blessed Sacrament with him. The person should be asked if he would first like to receive the sacrament of reconciliation before receiving Communion. If so the minister will tell the patient that he will ask the priest to stop by. If the priest is present with the group, this request should be given to the team priest as soon as possible while he is still in the hospital. If the priest does not come with the team and a referral has to be made, the patient should be given a definite time when the priest will come. This should be worked out beforehand with the priest so that the pastoral minister does not leave the person waiting for the priest who may not arrive until the next day.

As the pastoral minister makes his rounds, he should make a list of particular persons the team should pray for during the week—for example, people away from the sacraments, people undergoing surgery, the seriously ill, special requests, and special needs. This list should be shared with the others on the team in their final meeting before leaving the hospital.

When a patient is to receive the sacrament of anointing of the sick, the pastoral minister assigned to the floor should celebrate the sacrament with the priest and patient. The pastoral minister will share his book "Rite of Anointing and Pastoral Care of the Sick" with the patient so that he may more fully share in the sacrament. This book is the new ritual for the care of the sick and can be purchased at any Catholic book store. The parish priest will know where to buy it. The pastoral minister can help patients prepare to receive the sacrament of anointing by explaining the sacrament and perhaps praying with the person. If the person has been away from the Church for a long time, he may not be familiar with the way things are done now. Talk over the procedure with the team priest.

When the visitation is finished, the team should meet before leaving the hospital. At this time the Eucharist is returned to the person who will return the Blessed Sacrament to the church. Particular patients and needs should be shared and recorded by each team member. Each member will make a master list. These patients and their needs will be prayed for during the week by the team. Each member takes this responsibility upon himself. The team offers a prayer thanking the Lord for using them to bring his healing presence to so many persons in need.

The manager will reaffirm the meeting at the hospital for the following week. Changes may be suggested by the time of the year, holidays or members not able to attend. Major holidays may be times when the team would particularly like to visit. Back-up ministers should be available.

This mission and ministry of the team are carried out in an institution which follows very definite, special and unique procedures. A hospital brings to bear all the facilities and talents of different specialists into a health care team, of which the pastoral minister is an essential part. He should be prepared by special training to exercise his ministry within the framework of a particular institution. He must become part of the fabric which knits together the varied personnel of the hospital into a vital, healing, health team. Therefore it would be wise for the pastoral minister to have a knowledge of the hospital administration, procedures, goals and policies. He should be acquainted with aspects of patient care which involve the theology of sickness. He should know about Jesus' sacraments, a psychology of sickness, basic medical terminology, and the inter-relationships of the members of the health team. The hospital personnel should be made aware of the nature of the ministry of the pastoral minister and his role in relation to the physical, psychological and spiritual health of the patient.

This kind of ministry will require service, availability, dedication, knowledge, expertise, and, finally, a sense of commission—being sent forth by ecclesiastical authority to minister in the name of the body.

A knowledge of the hospital, the staff, the patients and their problems will help the minister to have an effective ministry. Someone beginning in pastoral care may find these suggestions helpful. They may serve as a very practical guide in serving the sick whether in the hospital, nursing home or at home.

Know the Administration and Staff

Pastoral ministers should be recognized and their ministry completely understood by the administration, by the professional staff, and by the patients. They should meet the administrator, the director of nurses, the director of social service and pertinent hospital personnel with whom they will be working. Hospital personnel are becoming aware of the advantages of having specially qualified ministers provide pastoral care, with all that this service means to patients in terms of their sickness.

The hospital can be an awesome place. The efficiency and professionalism of the personnel can sometimes become an obstacle to a person unsure of himself. The pastoral minister should familiarize himself with the usual procedures he will encounter. This will make him more comfortable in his relationships with staff and patients. He must know his ministry and how to exercise it in harmony with the varied disciplines he encounters.

A Vehicle of Grace

The pastoral minister must be conscious of the Spirit using him as the vehicle by which the Lord may be touching a person in his sickness. Many times the Lord will use the occasion of a hospital visit for his grace to touch a person who has been away from the sacraments for many years. The religious or lay person is often the direct occasion for a person to open up to the Lord when he would never do so with a priest.

The Female Face of God

Sometimes the femaleness of the pastoral minister with her overtones of gentleness, kindness and considerateness provides an atmosphere for the female face of God to touch the heart of the sick person.

Many times the Lord, using the femaleness of a pastoral minister, will soothe and heal past hurts in a person's life. The Lord can also use her as an intermediary in bringing the person to the point of forgiveness and reconciliation.

The pastoral minister must always be conscious of his or her own uniqueness and individuality. It is through this uniqueness and individuality that the Lord touches the lives of people.

Don't Push the Sacraments

The pastoral minister should never push sacraments or force his ministry upon anyone. The Lord Jesus frees, heals, makes whole, and saves in his time. The important thing is not a "one shot" reception of the sacraments but rather a conversion of heart.

Keep the Visit Pastoral

A visit must always be kept pastoral. No one, no matter how long he works with the sick, should become a pseudo-physician. People discuss their medical problems merely to look for reassurance that everything will be all right. They are not looking for a description of a similar operation or a story about a person with a similar disease. The pastoral minister is not qualified to give medical advice and should never offer a diagnosis or medical opinion. Neither should the pastoral minister tell patients of information learned through the medical staff or hospital charts.

Be Observant

When entering a sick room the pastoral minister will learn much about a patient by observing the various articles surrounding the person: religious articles, get-well cards from friends, flowers, types of magazines, reading material. Many times these articles will indicate attitudes which people have toward God and whether they have friends and visitors.

Know the Hospital Schedule

The pastoral minister should acquaint himself with the hospital schedule: in particular, times when patients are being bathed or given other care by nurses, doctors' rounds, nurses' scheduled care of patients, changes in personnel, meals and visiting hours. Usually patients are being bathed between 8:30 A.M. and 10:30 A.M. During this time the pastoral minister could be very much in the way. It is suggested that the pastoral minister stop by the nurses' station to let them know he is on the floor. This helps to concretize the working relationship between the pastoral minister and the total health team.

Be Open to All, But Respect Privacy

The pastoral minister should always greet every person in the room he visits regardless of religious beliefs. He should not merely visit Catholic patients. He should be open to ministering through prayer and other forms of ministry to patients of other religious beliefs. No patient should feel that the pastoral minister is in any way proselytizing. He should merely assure the person of his good wishes and prayers for his recovery.

If a patient indicates through his manner, gesture or even vocally that he does not wish the pastoral minister to visit him, talk with him or in any way come near him, the patient's wishes should be fully respected, even if this patient professes the Catholic faith. The role of the pastoral minister is to bring the healing Jesus to those wishing to encounter him. A person enters a hospital in order to receive physical healing through the health facility of which the pastoral minister is a part. He comes to be healed of his physical illness, not primarily to be converted. Many, many times the Lord Jesus— just as he uses the health facility and the talents of the professionals to bring physical healing—uses the same sickness to open a person to the healing presence of himself, manifested through the presence and ministry of the pastoral minister.

Sometimes people of other religious persuasions, especially Jehovah Witnesses, may attempt to engage the minister into an argumentative discussion. Avoid this in as friendly a manner as possible.

Make Visits Brief

A pastoral visit ordinarily should not be more than five minutes. Patients tire very easily and should not be overtaxed, especially in the intensive care and coronary care units. A more lengthy visit would be an exception, depending upon circumstances. For example, a counseling situation would need a longer visit.

Reassure—Don't Criticize

Sick people are looking for reassurances as to the quality of the hospital, their medical treatment, and their recovery from their sickness. Never under any circumstances become involved in criticizing or supporting criticism of the hospital or its staff.

Observe Signs

Care should be taken that the pastoral minister does not endanger himself or the patient by not observing warning signs. He should familiarize himself with common meanings of the signs N.P.O. (nothing by mouth) and Isolation (safeguards needed to protect patient). Check with the nurse to learn the isolation technique. The pastoral minister should always wash his hands if he has touched anyone or anything in isolation before going to the next patient. Always wash before leaving the hospital.

Identification

It is strongly recommended that the pastoral minister wear a bakelite pin nameplate with white lettering engraved with his name and the title "Catholic Pastoral Care."

Traumatic Experiences

Certain operations such as mastectomies, hysterectomies and amputations can cause tremendous anxieties and fears in patients. The pastoral minister should be aware of the traumatic experiences people undergo when faced with the loss of a body organ. Fears of disfiguration, loss, non-acceptance, and rejection sometimes have to be dealt with in helping people face realities. People face these situations according to where they are spiritually, who they are in relation to their family, whether they are married or single, old or young, and even whether they can expect support from the people who are closest to them. In handling these problems each person must be dealt with in the totality of his own personality and background. There is no book answer to the situation.

Know the Church's Teaching

The pastoral minister should be very much aware of the Church's position concerning abortion, tubal ligation and vasectomy. He should be able to discuss competently the psychological dimensions of these particular problems as they affect a person's future life.

Don't Pry or Be Nosy

Care should be taken at all times not to pry into people's lives or to push people to reveal matters they do not want to bring up at this time. The pastoral minister should avoid at all cost the tendency to be "nosy." People should always be free to discuss problems or not to discuss them as they so wish and not as the minister might think they should.

Alcoholism

The problem of alcoholism is not always limited to an alcoholic ward. At any given time in a total hospital census as many as ten percent of the patients could be alcoholics. This is an added consideration which may not be immediately obvious.

Special Units

There are some floors and special units that need particular training for all hospital personnel, including the pastoral minister. These units are: Intensive Care Unit (ICU), Coronary Care Unit (CCU), Burn Unit, Dialysis Unit, Premature Unit, and Pulmonary Unit. Special floors are Psychiatric, Pediatric, Geriatric, Gynecology—Obstetrics, and Maternity.

Intensive Care Unit (ICU). The patient in this unit is under unique distress. The minister must be brief, decisive and extremely gentle. He must never approach a bed hurriedly. He must first make sure that the patient realizes his presence before approaching him. To startle a person under such stress could trigger a series of problems in the patient. The pastoral minister must have at least a basic knowledge of the equipment used in the ICU. The doctors and nurses in this unit work as a team and the minister should be acquainted with each person's responsibility in the event of a crisis situation. At times the pastoral minister will find it necessary to calm other patients while the unit team is providing medical care to a patient in difficulty.

Coronary Care Unit (CCU). The heart unit has its own special problems. These patients have suffered extreme and excruciating pain and very much fear its reoccurrence. These patients frequently see the patient in the next bed die of the same problems they are suffering from. They live day by day with crisis situations occurring all around them.

The families of heart patients need tremendous encouragement as to the possibilities of carrying on their life as it was before. The heart patient needs to be reassured that when he gets well his activities need not be stopped or even curtailed but the same things can and will be able to be accomplished, but at a much slower, more peaceful and less anxious pace. Most patients in this unit are admitted under an emergency situation where everything they have been doing came to an abrupt halt. Sometimes upon recovery a complete change in both life style and job will be necessary. The pastoral minister ought not to presume to answer the patient's questions concerning his future activities. It is much better that the pastoral minister urge the patient to ask these questions of the doctor caring for him.

Dialysis Unit. Patients who enter this unit are usually outpatients. They come to the unit three times a week to be placed on a dialysis machine from three to five hours. Usually this process is used when a kidney transplant is either unavailable or otherwise impossible.

Patients who enter the unit and do not receive a kidney transplant fail in health over a period of three to five years and eventually die. At best, the dialysis machine can extract only a certain amount of impurities each time. There is nothing as perfect as the human kidney in taking care of waste material in the body. There is a real and genuine ministry that could be performed in this unit both to patients who must spend so much time just being there and to their families who see them gradually getting worse. Many times kidney patients have a strong tendency to commit suicide. It is by no means a unit to which untrained ministers should venture.

Burn Unit. This unit has problems of sight, smell and touch. There are usually no mirrors permitted. The smell in these units is something that the pastoral minister may find difficult to bear. Depending upon the severity of the burns, especially of the face, the patient is particularly anxious about the scars that will be left as he heals. He is also bothered by the tremendous pain involved in the least movement. He sometimes becomes violent when nurses approach him for his daily bath, at which time all loosened skin must be removed. The burn patient is never without pain.

Burn patients often blame their suffering on the care being given them by the staff. Sometimes they become personal and vocal in expressing their feelings. Many times the most professional and highly motivated nurses and doctors request to be transferred to another unit, at least for a period of time, after they have worked in this unit.

The families of these patients certainly need tremendous help as they see their loved ones suffering minute by minute, day by day, and many times month after month.

The pastoral minister should support the family by being present to them when they visit and offer support by words of encouragement or any other practical help the family may seek. Sometimes the family does not know exactly whom to ask to receive progress reports on their loved ones. Disfigurement and sometimes death will have to be faced by the family. Much support will be needed from the pastoral minister.

Pulmonary Unit. Patients in the pulmonary unit are suffering with diseases such as tuberculosis, pneumonia, collapsed lungs, emphysema, lung cancer, cystic fibrosis, asthma and other lung problems. Many hospitals use the pulmonary unit for people awaiting lung surgery. It is important to be familiar with the various machines used in this unit, many of which will also be found in other units and on the floors. People in this unit are under extreme stress, mainly because of the extreme difficulty in trying to breathe. Discouragement is especially prevalent in people with chronic conditions. The struggle to breathe can change the entire personality of a person.

Sometimes the drugs used cause people's hair to fall out. This is an especially acute problem for teenage girls and needs to be handled very gently, but with the reassurance that it is only temporary. In this instance, the pastoral minister can work together with the staff.

Premature Unit. The premature unit of a particular hospital may service the premature babies of other hospitals in the area. Some hospitals have a special ambulance equipped just for this purpose. Most of the work of the pastoral minister will be with the parents of these children. If the mother and baby are in the same hospital, it would be wise for the pastoral minister to visit the mother to show interest and to reassure her if the child is progressing favorably. Under no circumstances should the pastoral minister offer medical information or give false hope when the child is doing poorly. Most of the problems in the premature unit are pulmonary problems which can very easily go either way at any moment.

Psychiatric Wards. Unless the pastoral minister is a priest or someone specially trained in psychology or psychiatry, he should under no circumstances presume to enter this ward. He could do untold harm and even permanent damage if he does not know what he is doing. In other words—keep out!

Pediatrics. One of the most difficult wards in any hospital is the pediatric ward. It can be a most pleasant and enjoyable experience and at the same time be a most frustrating and heart-rending experience.

Children can be there for a variety of reasons, from child abuse and child molestation to cystic fibrosis and cancer. The problems on this ward are always linked and compounded with the human problems of the parents and rest of the family.

The pastoral minister must always be aware of and consider the parents' attitudes and feelings while their child is sick. He must also respect the feelings and wishes of the child's parents in matters of religion. The pastoral minister should never under any circumstances ignore the parents or relatives of sick children.

Many of the more modern hospitals have made provision for one of the parents to stay in the same room overnight with their child. This sometimes affords the minister an opportunity to sit with the parent in a more relaxed situation.

Geriatrics Ward. Extended care facilities have a large number of elderly patients who must stay there until they have fully recuperated because they are from nursing homes or homes for adults. The relatives have either died or do not bother with them. Most of their friends have died or are incapacitated themselves and cannot visit. And so the geriatrics ward is a very lonely place. Many people must spend a number of months in this ward, with no visitors or anyone with whom to share their problems. On leaving the wards they return to an equally lonely place and existence, the nursing home. One of the biggest physical problems these elderly people can face is poor circulation resulting from diabetes, which often requires amputation. This confines patients to wheelchairs, further limiting their already tiny world. It is the exception when chronically sick elderly patients do not feel useless and unwanted and that no one really cares whether they exist or not. Many patients merely sit around waiting to die and sometimes honestly wish that they would.

Nursing home patients who depend upon medicaid frequently are not sent back to the same nursing home at the end of their hospital stay. If they are sent back, they may not return to the same room and many times not even to the same floor. This causes much anxiety, fear, and a sense of hopelessness. New York City has thousands of elderly people who have no human ties, no sense of belonging, and who in reality are human beings without home or roots anywhere.

In the geriatric ward, the pastoral minister will have to prove himself or herself as a caring, honest, straightforward person who is not trying to manipulate people. Like children, the elderly can see through phoniness immediately. These elderly people have reasons not to be trusting. The pastoral minister must prove that he or she is worthy to be trusted.

Elderly people have very much to contribute, even if only from their years of experience. They have been down many, many streets. They should not be talked to or treated as children. They have every right to tell anyone treating them as such to go away.

Gynecology—Obstetrics. This is often a difficult

ward for the pastoral minister. He must have a very
clear-cut knowledge of the Church's teachings on abortion, tubal ligation and birth control. He will encounter
all the diseases which can affect women, many of which
may be cause for debilitating surgery. He must be very
gentle in his approach to patients in this ward, especially if he is a male minister. It takes a very special person
to begin to understand what it must be like and how a
patient would feel encountering a hysterectomy. Often
the pastoral minister will have to deal with patients
who are suffering from complications resulting from a
recent abortion.

The pastoral minister must be aware of the hor-
monal changes which take place as a result of a hysterectomy. These changes, similar to the changes of
menopause, can result in a total personality change or
periods of depression. Very often this ward will have
terminal cancer patients. The pastoral minister must be
sensitive and discerning, since he may be dealing with a
patient who is not aware of her terminal illness.

Maternity. This ward has been called by hospital
personnel and many others the "happy ward."
Everyone is happy when a child is born healthy and
vibrant. But frequently this is not the case. Stillborns,
deformed or mentally retarded babies, children with
cystic fibrosis, spastics, and babies with pulmonary
problems and many other difficulties are born to
parents in this ward. Sometimes it takes a special inge-
nuity and balance to be able to assist the staff in helping the parents to cope with these extremely difficult
situations. The pastoral minister ought to be very cau-
tious of offering advice and solutions to problems which
will be with the parents for a long time after he has
gone. He should not presume to enter into the situation

if he is not very familiar with the condition with which a child has been born.

Maternity wards have special hours and times when visitors can be on the floors. The pastoral minister must adhere to the schedules. He should not be surprised if he is restricted by the nursing staff if he tries to enter the ward at other than the specified times.

Hygiene

The hospital, being a place where people come with a variety of diseases, can become a source of danger to the untrained and careless pastoral minister. Doctors, nurses and staff are trained to wear clothing that can be discarded or easily washed. All hospital personnel are trained to wash their hands with a disinfectant soap before leaving the hospital or before eating in the hospital cafeteria or anywhere else. Sinks, soap and towels are available in all rooms, wards, and units where it will be necessary to wash one's hands before leaving. The pastoral minister should be careful as he moves about the hospital not to carry diseases from one person to the next. Lastly, he should under no condition presume to go to the hospital if he has a cold, has just recovered from the flu, or has any disease that he could transmit to a patient. People in hospitals are in very weakened conditions and extremely prone to contact diseases.

Visiting the Blind

When visiting a blind person or someone who has very little sight, the pastoral minister should always identify himself immediately upon entering the room. The pastoral minister should also realize that the person is blind, not deaf. He should always speak directly to the patient, not through someone else. He should never hesitate to use the same words he would use with a sighted person, words such as "see, saw, eyes, look out for, watch out." While in the room the pastoral minister should never change the position of any of the furniture or anything the person may have on his night table. This could cause much difficulty for the blind person. In giving directions to a blind person, give them as clearly as possible according to the way he is facing. Use words such as "your left, your right, your front, your back." If the pastoral minister has occasion to assist the blind person into a chair or wheelchair, he should put the blind person's hand on the back of the chair so that the patient will be able to seat himself much more easily.

If the minister is there during mealtime, he should tell the person what is on the tray, telling him the position of the food by using the face of a clock. The closest item to him would be six o'clock, the farthest from him would be twelve o'clock, things on his right would be three o'clock, things on his left would be nine o'clock.

If the pastoral minister has occasion to lead a blind person for a walk, he should let the blind person take his arm. He should never take the blind person's arm or put a hand on his back while walking. This gives a blind person the impression that he is being pushed. If presented with an obstacle such as a doorway, steps, a table or chair, or turning a corner, the pastoral minister should make sure that he describes the situation before reaching it. His movement will indicate to the blind person what action should be taken.

Visiting the Hard of Hearing

The hard-of-hearing person requires much patience on the part of the pastoral minister, who must realize that what he is saying could be easily misunderstood, misconstrued, and sometimes not even heard. The hard-of-hearing person may give the impression that he really understands. He may be taking his cues from facial expressions and gestures so as not to admit that he really has a problem.

So as not to embarrass people the pastoral minister ought to follow a few very simple directions. He should always face the person he is speaking with. He should not speak to anyone who is facing away. He should speak normally and never mouth his words. He should not speak while eating, chewing gum, or smoking, since these things usually make hearing difficult and lip-reading impossible. He should keep his hands away from his mouth for the same reasons. He should never speak to a deaf person who is not visible to him. If a deaf person is having difficulty understanding a complicated phrase, the pastoral minister should try to rephrase it, not keep repeating the same words. The hard-of-hearing should be treated as normal people with a hearing defect.

Patients' Modesty

Sometimes the ordinary precautions concerning modesty are abandoned by patients who are very sick, or recovering from surgery, or senile. The pastoral minister may find himself or herself entering a room or ward where some patient is uncovered. He has either of two things to do—turn around and run out or realize that he is part of the hospital team and therefore size up the situation. Many times the nurse is unaware of the problem; many times the patient keeps kicking off bedclothes. The pastoral minister should report the situation to the nurse but should consider the matter a mere occupational hazard. He should under no circumstances become flustered and upset. Sometimes patients will use their hospital situation to expose themselves deliberately or to make some gesture. The pastoral minister should size up the situation and handle the matter in as practical a way as he judges necessary. Sometimes the practical way may be to ignore the gesture and the patient.

Unusual Requests

The pastoral minister will find that his affiliation with the Church will engender many requests that would not be made of other hospital personnel. He may be asked to get the patient an aspirin. He may be asked to carry the patient's criticism or complaints to the administration. He may be asked to register a complaint against the hospital. He may be asked to find out and inform the patient of the doctor's diagnosis and prognosis. He may be asked to help the patient in and out of bed. He may be asked for water, pills, candy, cigarettes, chewing gum and the like. The pastoral minister must be concerned with pastoral ministry and not take on the role of any other hospital personnel. He must be on his guard that whatever he does in his ministry is not against the doctor's orders and in no way jeopardizes the person's health. He must perform his ministry and refer all other matters to the responsible personnel.

Essential to the pastoral minister is his willingness to learn from those with whom he serves, from his own experience and from the sick through whom Jesus teaches all of us how to serve his body.

11
Ministry to Nursing Homes, Health-Related Facilities and Adult Homes

Have you ever experienced the feeling of emptiness, the feeling that you are truly alone in the midst of a crowd, a sense of isolation which gradually creeps in on you because you do not hear so well, or see so well, or move as quickly or are as steady on your feet as you used to be? Have you ever wanted to be independent yet had to depend upon someone else to cook your meals, push your wheelchair, feed you because your hands are crippled with arthritis? Have you ever sat hour after hour watching other people living while you are just waiting for the next activity? Have you hoped that perhaps one person might truly be your friend, someone who would care for you and like you as you are—someone who would come to see you and talk with you, who would treat you as an equal, who would share his or her life with you and you would share your life with him or her?

Have you ever wanted to shout that you haven't died, that you're living, that you have the same feelings as everyone else, that you want to be loved, that you want to love, that you want someone who cares about you, that you want to care about someone?

If you had these experiences, then you may be one of many people who live in our institutions for the elderly, or a shut-in sitting behind the curtain of a window in a split-level suburban home, or behind the locked and bolted door of a room in a tenement project, apartment or hotel, afraid to go out.

Your Church, Jesus, must seek you out where you are. It must reach out to you to free you from your bonds of loneliness. The human Jesus, we your people, must go into the streets. We must make you feel a part of our Christian community. We must see past that huge building and see you waiting. We must begin to see you as an integral part of our parish life. We have a lot of growing to do, a lot of forgetfulness of you for which we must be forgiven. We must as priests ask to be forgiven for putting you on the shelf when you grow old, for not being open and not accepting you as a real part of the parish life just because you live in a big building and you cannot come to our big buildings. We must be forgiven for bringing you the Eucharist only once a month when you were in the habit of daily Mass, for being opposed to lay people sharing ministry with us, for not having the courage to change, to reach out, for shutting our minds and hearts to your cries, for placing ourselves in our own tombs of isolation. Jesus, free us. Help us to be free. Help us to be free so we can truly free others.

We must, as religious, ask you to forgive us for our isolation and caring so much about ourselves, for being closed to your shouts for closeness, for being so interested in getting to another meeting to talk about the needs of the sick, elderly and handicapped that we forget to visit you and ask you what you need. We must learn to become Jesus in this world. Ah yes, but to whom?

We must as laity ask you to forgive us for isolating you. We have our prayer meetings, our Masses, our societies, our encounters, our workshops, our lectures, our church. We pass by your building nearly every day. In fact, we don't even see your building anymore. It sort of blends into the neighborhood; you have become one of the faceless other humans that we pass each day. It's the priest's job, anyway, to visit you. He has more time. What does he do all day? We're very busy. Jesus never had a family to take care of. He didn't have to wash clothes, cook, shop, or go to the office all day. Besides, we just want to relax and watch television. Let someone else do it. You'll have to forgive us for these attitudes. We are learning.

The key to the pastoral care of the elderly is the fostering and development of lasting and permanent relationships. Unlike the hospital where relationships are temporary, the relationship established with an elderly person is no different than any other relationship. The emphasis is upon the person, not his or her age.

The pastoral minister must develop this attitude. Rather than say: "I am going to visit one of the residents at the nursing home," he should think: "Tim is my friend, he lives at the Nursing Home. I want to stop by and say hello and tell him what happened to me the other day. I want to see how he's feeling." The pastoral minister must care for people as persons.

If we visit people in residences or nursing homes in groups, we tend to avoid individual relationships. It is better that one person visits a particular person or few persons, treating people as individuals.

When we live in institutions, of necessity, we are forced to live according to a clock. There is a time to get up, a time to eat, a time to sit, a time to walk, a time to go to bed, a time to watch television, a time for activities, a time for whatever. By and large we do not have much privacy. The pastoral visitor must always be conscious that he is in someone else's home. He is the guest. People ought to have the right to accept the visitor into his or her life or not.

When our life styles change, we experience many times a loss of role. When a husband dies, a wife becomes a widow. When a wife dies, a husband becomes a widower. A person passes from being a worker to being retired. When parents die, children become orphans. Our relationships and life styles are changing all the time. Persons should be accepted as they are. No one can totally compensate for the loss of someone or something. He can only give to the newness of the relationship as it exists now. He need only be himself and permit his friend to be himself.

Perhaps the most important quality in a pastoral minister is common sense. When a young person forgets something, we say that he has a lot on his mind. When an elderly person forgets something, we say he has hardening of the arteries. When a young person gets angry about something, we say that he is exerting his independence. When an elderly person gets annoyed about something, we say that he is unreasonable. When a young person looks for affection, we say that he is sowing his oats. When an elderly person looks for affection, we say he ought to have more sense. When a young person does not want to change, we call him conservative. When an elderly person does not want to change, we say he is obstinate. When a young person doesn't attend church, we say that the liturgy is not relevant. When an elderly person doesn't attend church, we say he has a problem.

Pastoral ministers have to be open to the possibility that some people may regularly visit Jesus in the

Eucharist but have real problems about being in a small chapel with a large group of people. We must teach people to love Jesus as a friend and constant companion.

If elderly people do not trust you, don't be surprised. Our society has conditioned us to expect people to "rip us off." Don't blame elderly people for being suspicious. If they trust you at first contact, you may even refer to them as gullible.

Many of the things we accuse other people of, whether we are young or old, reflect our own particular "hang-up." If you are youth orientated, you may not want to go near the elderly because you fear losing your youth. If you are middle-aged, you may shun the elderly because you may have a fear of growing old. If you are elderly, you may want to associate with younger people so that you may feel younger. Rot! Be whatever you are. You cannot be something that you are not.

A lifetime can mean something quite different to each of us. I have seen children die of cancer, cystic fibrosis, and heart attacks at the age of two and three. I have witnessed and shared the death of people at the ages of ninety-two and ninety-three from the same diseases. I don't know why. The only difference was experience and awareness. Somehow the two-year-old was asking the same question as the ninety-two-year-old.

Don't be afraid to visit old people. Don't wonder what you will say or how you will say it. People are people. Folks will share with you, whatever you can do to help. If a person becomes your friend, maybe you may be asked to water her plant, or write a letter to her daughter who hasn't visited her in five years.

The best advice I can give is to be yourself. Use your common sense. Jesus was himself. If you were sick or elderly or handicapped, how would you want people to treat you? Jesus gave the answer to our dealings with everyone. "Do unto others as you would have them do unto you. Love your neighbor as you would want him to love you."

Involving people in certain things they can help you with gives people a sense of being wanted. It provides them with a sense of usefulness. It can take the form of filling envelopes, making rosaries for the sick, praying for the needs of someone else, becoming a friend of someone else in the home, being responsible for the music ministry for the Mass celebrated at the home, taking care of the altar linens, or setting up the altar. People want to be part of the giving rather than always the getting.

The pastoral visitor need not make lengthy visits. A brief visit once a week, if consistent, is more important than lengthy irregular visits. One should want to visit because he enjoys the company of the person visited. Duty never produces friendship. Caring does.

Remembering someone's birthday, anniversary, and special days such as Christmas, Easter and Valentine Day is important. Remembering to send a postcard while away on vacation can be terribly exciting and very warm.

The type and style of pastoral care to be given at a nursing home, at a health-related facility or an adult home will differ according to the particular needs of the residents.

A nursing home provides medical care and skilled nursing care at the bedside around the clock. A health-related facility provides an infirmary with skilled nursing care and visiting doctors. An adult residence does not provide any medical care.

Each of these institutions has people who need supportive services. People in nursing homes need total

supportive services. People in health-related facilities
are more or less ambulatory and need supportive services to a degree. People in adult residences can usually
take care of themselves. Their supportive services might
be prepared meals, laundry, cleaning of rooms, making
beds—similar to services that a hotel would provide.

The needs of the people in each of these kind of institutions will differ greatly. Some adult residences accept people from mental institutions who have had his-
tories of mental disorders. These people need more help
than a visit from a pastoral minister. Other homes for
adults accept retarded people and handicapped people.
This creates still other problems.

A parish reaching out to an institution must determine what sort of institution it is. What sort of people
live there, and the specific needs the parish ministers
can meet and the parish wants to meet.

As a beginning, the pastor, one of his associates or
a group should visit the institution. He or they should
meet with the administrator or the person in charge.
They should discuss the institution and the expectations
of the administrator. The researcher should study the
institution and take time to evaluate his findings. The
results should be brought to the people who intend to
reach out as ministers. The pastor should recognize that
this institution has parishioners who are in need of a
service. What is the difference between residents who
live in an institution and residents who live in apart-
ments or private houses in his parish? Are the institutionalized any less his parishioners? Maybe we should
begin to ask ourselves, "What, or rather who, is a
parishioner?"

Persons in nursing homes, health-related facilities
or homes for adults should have the opportunity of
receiving the Eucharist as often as possible. Those for-

tunate enough to be able to come to church must be aware of those who are unable to come. The parish should be concerned with all its parishioners.

Mass should be celebrated at least once a week for residents of nursing homes and health-related facilities. If the priest cannot go, then he should arrange for a eucharistic service conducted by extraordinary ministers of the Eucharist.

Each institution in a parish should be researched and studied. Needs should be evaluated. Priorities should be set. The people of the parish should determine the needs and respond accordingly.

12
Yes, Lord!

If you desire to be a pastoral minister you must first say "yes" to the Lord. You must be willing to be a disciple. A disciple is not someone who does things for other people. He is a person who has formed a true relationship with the Lord. He is a person who has declared within himself that Jesus is the Lord of his life. He is willing to let the Lord transform him into the sort of person God wants him to become. He is in a state of becoming, a state of transformation, a state of being open to the Spirit in his life. He has accepted Jesus as his Savior and brother. He has said "yes."

He is willing to touch the spirit of Mary who offered her very person to the Father so that his Son could be born into the world and touch mankind with his flesh. He is ready to become Jesus to his brothers and sisters. He realizes that he will be asked to bring to birth the Lord Jesus in the lives of his brothers and sisters.

Jesus is alive in his body today. The pastoral minister hears his call. He is willing to say "yes." He is willing to let the Lord use him to free his fellow man. He is willing to let the Lord free him from the many darknesses within himself and is open to the Lord using him to dispell the darkness in others.

He is willing to say "yes" to the Lord. He excludes no one from the possibility of his ministry. He realizes that the Lord Jesus died and rose from death for everyone. Every person has been cleansed by the blood of the Lord. Every person is the recipient of the Lord's love.

We must step out to feed the hungry, give drink to the thirsty, clothe the naked, give shelter to the homeless, free those in the bondage of loneliness, anxiety, fear, and resentments. We must step out to say "yes" to the Lord and say "yes" to our brothers and sisters when they reach out their hands to us.

When we touch the life of another human being with the touch of the Lord's life, we give birth to his presence in our fellow man.

I could not help thinking recently, while Sister Julie and I were visiting the City Shelter for Homeless Men in Manhattan, that these men were my brothers, that they were members of the Lord's body in need of healing, not amputation. Society has amputated them. I feel that we must treat the disease until the Lord decides that the pain and struggle are too much for the human spirit to withstand. Only when the Lord decides that his journey in this life is ended can we rest from sharing the Lord with our brother in so desperate a need.

If we wish to minister to others, we should never consider the cost. The true minister reaches out, knowing that he must give a part of himself away to his brother or sister, that in giving to another he must die and rise with the Lord. The Christian who wants to be the Lord's disciple must live as Jesus did. Jesus reached out, not considering the cost; he reached out to his fellow man so that he could bring him to his Father. He died in the attempt. By the power of the Father he rose.

There is a story told of a young man who couldn't bring himself to believe in all this "Jesus stuff." He and his wife lived in farm country in a small house he had built with his own hands. He was a beautiful young man, filled with compassion for his fellow man. No stranger ever came to his door without being welcomed and invited to eat. He just couldn't bring himself to go to church or join any church. He believed in God but preferred to say his prayers in private. All this talk about Jesus being the Son of God and becoming man, a human being like us, was just too much.

One Christmas eve his wife pleaded with him to come to Midnight Mass with her. It was beginning to snow, and she felt that it would be nice to go to church together. He told her that he would rather not, that he would only feel like a hypocrite. So she went off to church with the neighbors who picked her up in their car.

She had been gone only a short while when he heard a thump against the house, then another thump and another and another. He looked out the window and saw that the snow had become very heavy. It was becoming very difficult to even see the light in the tiny window of his barn where his cow and a few chickens spent the winter.

He put on his coat and went outside to investigate the thumping. To his surprise he saw a flock of birds who had been caught in the storm. The snow had collected on their wings and forced them to crash against his lighted window. His heart went out to the poor creatures as he watched them struggle to put to flight again. He ran into the house and brought back a huge sack. He tried in vain to catch the birds and put them in the sack so he could bring them from the freezing snow into the warmth of his house. The more he tried, the more the birds scurried away from him. They were frightened of the immensity of their benefactor. The more he shouted that he wanted to help, the more they ran to get away.

"I know," he said. "I will throw open the doors to my barn. I will light a light. Surely they will fly from the darkness and cold toward the light. Then they will be safe in my barn and be warm."

He quickly lighted a lamp and set it in the middle of the doorway. The barn was flooded with light. The cow stared out into the night. The chickens stepped and pecked their way around the barn.

But the birds would not go in. They came as far as the door but would not enter. They were afraid. Some even entered on the threshold but quickly returned into the darkness and cold. They could not take the step. The young man was beside himself.

"Why?" he cried. "I can save them. They need not die. Why won't they go into my barn? Why won't they trust me? I can bring them to the warmth of my barn so they can survive. They can't survive without me. Why? Why?"

Suddenly he began to realize that there was nothing he could do to help them. They were going to die, and he could do nothing but stand by and watch. The birds were afraid. They were afraid of him. He was too immense and they were so tiny.

"Why don't they understand? I only want to help them survive. I don't want to hurt them. Why don't they understand?" he thought to himself.

"If only they weren't afraid of me," he began to murmur. "If, if only I could become one of them, then they wouldn't be afraid. That's it—if only I could become one of them. If only I could become one of them. If only. . . ."

In the distance the silence of the night was broken by the ringing of the church bell. Its sound seemed to fill the hills with its silver tones. He paused, looked lovingly at the struggling birds. A tear trickled down his cheek. "If only. . . ." he muttered again. The church bell resounded throughout the mountainside. It was midnight. He fell to his knees in the snow. He knelt for a long time, his head bowed. "Yes, Lord!"

13
Structuring a Parish Pastoral Care Program

The structure of a pastoral care program will depend largely upon what needs are to be met and what priorities are decided upon. One parish may observe how another parish has structured its program and find that the model is one which could be used again. I feel that each parish should structure itself in a style that is comfortable to those managing it. It should be functionable and manageable. It should be structured to efficiently and effectively accomplish its goals. Its structure should be flexible enough that it may admit change when necessary. Most important is that the people involved agree that the organization is only a vehicle which serves them and that they do not exist merely to serve the organization. The dynamism comes from a knowledge of the importance of each individual. The Father loves each of us equally, each and every one of us. The structure should help the body to become one in faith, one in hope, one in love. This is vital to growth, both personally and together.

I offer the following four models which may help a parish wishing to begin or having already begun to restructure its program. There can be as many ways of structuring as there are parishes with people in need.

93

Model Number One

Saint Gerard Majella's Parish in Hollis, New York has four large institutions and many homebound sick, elderly and handicapped. It serves a hospital with one hundred and fifty beds and three nursing homes with a total of one thousand beds. The program has involved three priests, religious, students from the local college seminary, and lay people, including many teenagers. Some of the lay people and religious were chosen and commissioned as extraordinary ministers of the Eucharist.

One of the associate pastors oversees the program. Two volunteer lay persons act as coordinating managers for the entire group. Each of the groups ministering to the four institutions has a manager, and the group ministering to the homebound has a manager. These five individual managers meet with their particular ministers once a week to discuss the particular needs of the people within the institution for which they are responsible.

The managers of the five groups meet with the associate pastor and the two coordinating managers once a month to discuss progress, problems, needs of the ministers and relationships among the groups (hospitalized person returning home and needing continued ministry as a homebound person, or a homebound person entering the hospital or nursing home). These types of problems are discussed and a method of communication decided upon.

The entire group meets together as the body of the Lord twice a month. One meeting is for the purpose of spiritual growth. The time is spent in prayer, Scripture reading, sharing what the Lord is doing in their personal lives, a reading that has touched someone, personal witnessing to the Lord—whatever way the Spirit would inspire the meeting in prayer. The second meeting in the month is a business meeting where each manager of the individual groups would bring to the entire body the same things that were discussed within the individual groups. This brings cohesiveness to the group in the event that a member may switch in his or her ministry or new members join.

The coordinating managers conduct both general meetings. The priest is present as part of the group offering his special ministry to the group. He oversees the group, permitting the group to make responsible decisions on its own. One of the priests of the parish is part of each group and ministers in the group at the particular institution it serves. All share in the ministry to the homebound. Each of the nursing homes has a eucharistic service on Sunday morning conducted by the extraordinary ministers of the Eucharist. They also have the celebration of the Eucharist (Mass) twice a month. Pastoral ministers visit the residents at the homes during the week. Ministers are assigned particular floors to visit and "get to know" those people.

The hospital is visited each Tuesday afternoon for a complete visitation of all the patients. Two priests, a permanent deacon, two religious, and two lay persons visit the hospital as a Catholic pastoral care team. Everyone is visited bed to bed. Priests and pastoral ministers serve the hospital as a pastoral care team. Each member of the team is important and needed. The team serves as partners, as sharers in ministry.

Ministry is personalized. The sacraments are celebrated, and prayer is shared with patients who so wish. Each patient receiving Holy Communion is prayed with. The minister waits until the patient has swallowed the Blessed Sacrament, gives water to the patient if necessary, says the final prayer and blesses the person. If the person has some particular need or concern, this is mentioned in a special spontaneous prayer. Provision is made for persons requesting daily communion.

During the remainder of the week the priest answers all requests or calls from the hospital. On Sunday morning after the 10 o'clock parish Mass, eucharistic ministers bring Holy Communion to the hospital and also to the shut-ins around the parish.

The homebound are also visited once a week by pastoral ministers. During that visit the ministers pay a social call or try to meet the specific need of each person. That need may be simply a visit. Perhaps the minister needs to straighten up the house or to see any variety of needs.

Model Number Two

Sister Marie Lenihan, C.S.J., a full-time salaried person of Our Lady Queen of Martyrs Parish, Forest Hills, New York, is the manager of the parish pastoral care program. The parish has two large hospitals and three nursing homes within its boundaries. The neighborhood has a large elderly population and many shut-ins. The pastoral ministers uncovered many problems which needed the assistance of trained social workers.

The program there evolved with the appointment of a council of ministers from the volunteers who help the manager. The council consists of the managers of the various groups. Presently, there are seven groups. Each of the five institutions has a group of ministers who serve its people. Each has an associate manager who is part of the council and meets with the manager to coordinate the activities of all the groups.

Two additional groups have been formed. One group consists of Sunday ministers who bring Holy Communion to shut-ins. There are twelve ministers who bring Holy Communion to twenty-five parishioners who cannot come to the Eucharist at the parish church. Each minister celebrates the Eucharist with the shut-in by praying with the person, sharing Scripture, sharing the homily given by the priest at church and bringing the greetings of all in the parish to their brother or sister. The second additional group is a special group of people being trained by the Brooklyn Catholic Charities personnel of the Flushing Human Service Center. Two social workers from Catholic Charities reviews with the manager cases of people needing the help of social workers. The pastoral ministers are receiving instruction in basic social work from Catholic Charities of Brooklyn so that they may be able to make referrals and placements and obtain professional help for people when the circumstances so indicate.

Days of prayer, prayer together at meetings, and the spiritual development of the pastoral ministers are a priority in the program as it is developing. The program is open to new membership and gives volunteers a sense of becoming and worth.

This program is developing in such a manner that it will involve people of the parish in the ministry of clerical work, office management, and eventually parish homemakers (people who will cook a meal for someone, or clean a home once a week or whatever the need). One woman, a hairdresser, ministers to elderly people by spending Saturday mornings setting the hair of shut-ins. She serves two people each week. That's her gift. She also brings with it a lot of Tender Loving Care (T.L.C.).

Model Number Three

Twenty pastoral ministers from the local parishes, one priest and one sister service the Neponsit Home for the Aged in Neponsit, New York. There are three as-

sociate managers. One manager organizes and schedules eight ministers (husbands and wives) who conduct
eucharistic services on Sunday morning at 9:30 A.M. in
the Catholic chapel. At 9 o'clock another team (husband and wife) conduct a eucharistic service in a solarium in another building for people unable to come to
the chapel.

A volunteer pastoral minister is manager of the
pastoral minister volunteers who visit the residents at
the home once a week. The ministers have been assigned to sections of the institution. It is their responsibility to know the names of everyone in their section
and be able to report at the monthly meeting any problems or needs of these residents. The manager is also
responsible for scheduling the ministers who visit the
residents when they become hospitalized.

A volunteer pastoral minister is manager of the
service teams that conduct eucharistic services on Sunday morning in the chapel at the residence.

On Friday afternoons Mass is celebrated for the
residents. Music is played in the chapel for one hour
before services. Three eucharistic ministers bring the
Eucharist to those in the infirmary and to those unable
to come to the solarium or chapel.

The Mass in the chapel has full participation on
the part of the residents. One of the residents is lector,
two residents usher, and all take an active part in the
responses and song. All the new liturgies have been in-
augurated. Approximately every six weeks there is a
communal celebration of the anointing of the sick. The
people are invited to come forward to receive the sacrament.

The residents say the rosary together on Saturday
mornings. A charismatic prayer group of residents
meets after the rosary.

The ministers meet once a month for two hours to

pray and discuss the ministry. The director of social service at the home always attends this meeting. This way there is input from a staff member.

This is a typical agenda:

1. Index card for each resident with pertinent information.

2. Update residents: admissions and discharges.

3. Report about each floor section by visiting ministers. Success or problems with new arrangement of visitation. Special problems with or of certain residents.

4. Hospital ministry report.

5. Policy of giving gifts and other favors requested by residents or not requested.

6. Deaths and free burials.

7. Alcoholism and the residents.

8. Adopt a grandparent program.

9. Car insurance on cars of ministers who take residents shopping.

Some of the residents who are well enough visit one another when hospitalized. A few residents visit nursing homes in the area and volunteer at the local hospital in various programs.

The people have grown to love the pastoral ministers and their interest in coming to visit them. Often the ministers bring some of the residents to the local church for some special event. As much as possible the residents are involved in the activities of the home and neighborhood.

Model Number Four

What does a parish do when it has fourteen institutions within its boundaries? For many priests and people this would be an impossible task—but not to the priests, religious and laity at St. Mary's Star of the Sea in Far Rockaway, N.Y. With six nursing homes, four health-related facilities, four homes for adults and one hospital, this parish was faced with the challenge of bringing pastoral care to three thousand elderly people, special problems related to homes for adults, and a hospital with one hundred and fifty beds. The parish church burned down, has a full school capacity, and is in a neighborhood that is considered economically deprived.

Father James McKenna and his associates, Father John Regan, Charles Nichols and David O'Brien, are a unique group of priests. Sister Cathy Bott, who was hired by Father McKenna to head up a program of pastoral care to the homebound and the parishioners in these institutions, is as unique as the priests with whom she serves.

Sister Cathy speaks of "her priests" as the greatest in the world. She means it. When she speaks of them she calls them "my priests." I truly believe that they are. This parish has a spark about it that only a closeness of true friendship among its priests, sisters and laity could develop. One gets the impression that this parish is a true Christian community. Father McKenna is a unique priest. He knows his parish and gives freedom to those who serve in a way that lets the Lord use the special gifts of each person in the community.

Before Sister Cathy's coming, the priests of this parish reached out to the homebound and the institutionalized. Over the years the number of institutions increased, possibly because the area was a beach area and open to development. The pastor was equal to the challenge. He discerned the need for a pastoral person who would coordinate the ministry of the priests, the religious, and especially the laity who were becoming involved as pastoral visitors and extraordinary ministers of the Eucharist. The Lord guided his decisions, and Sister Cathy was hired.

The pastoral care is organized in the following fashion. Holy Mass is celebrated in each of the nursing homes and health-related facilities once a month. On Sundays a lay person conducts a eucharistic service for the residents.

During the week the residents of the homes and homebound are visited. Meetings of all the ministers are held every two weeks. Prayer is stressed by Sister Cathy as extremely important. Training and supervision are an integral part of the program. Days of prayer or recollection are part of the lives of the ministers.

The program is open to any parishioner willing to step forward. Stepping forward or reaching out is something the parishioner has to think about and decide for himself. No one's gift is refused. It is the parishioner who decides to reach out or not. There is a job for everyone.

The program includes a cross-section of parishioners. People from eight to eighty years of age are involved. Some of the people have been selected as extraordinary ministers of the Eucharist, some as pastoral ministers who visit the homebound or the institutionalized. Teenagers are involved with visitation, grade school children participate in "Adopt a Grandparent" programs, and pre-schoolers are involved when they visit along with their parents.

Professional back-up is provided by the Rockaway Mental Health Clinic, Catholic Charities Human Service Center, Rockaway Health Council, and professionals in the parish. The local police have been alerted to "keep an eye" on the residents of the homes when they go out.

14
The Ministers Speak

A book of this nature would not be complete without a final word from some of the pastoral ministers who have said "yes" to the Lord. The sick, elderly and handicapped taught me about themselves and how to minister to them. My association with the priests, religious and laity who stepped forward to serve their brothers and sisters has taught me through their dedication and obvious growth in the Spirit the meaning of team ministry. I no longer can minister in isolation. Those who share in the Lord's priesthood have taught me through the witness of their lives and service what it means to be part of his body as we together serve our brothers and sisters. I am indeed a very fortunate man, privileged to be sharing life with so many beautiful people. The person who comes to truly realize that things really don't matter but people do matter—that person is doubly blessed.

I have been blessed by those whom the Lord has sent into his fields to gather the harvest. He sent me into these same fields so that we would labor together to build his Kingdom.

Recently I asked some people to share why they volunteered to be pastoral ministers and how they carry out their ministry. Here are some of their replies.

Sister Marie Lenihan, C.S.J. has spent two years as the manager of the pastoral ministry at Our Lady Queen of Martyrs Parish in Forest Hills, N.Y. This witness of Sister Marie was given after a few months of ministry to the sick and elderly.

Recently Father Joseph M. Dolan asked me to share how I was led to become a parish coordinator of pastoral ministry to the sick and aged and how my pastoral ministry has evolved. This request gave me the opportunity to reflect on some recent developments in my life and has brought me once again to the conclusion that the Lord's ministry is definitely his own. We are carried along as he uses us to complete his work.

A few months ago I was a grammar school teacher involved in parish activities and becoming fragmented by the ever increasing demands of the dual ministry of teaching and parish work. During the summer of 1974 I enrolled in a course entitled "Pastoral Ministry of the Sick" which was given under the auspices of the Sisters' Senate of the Diocese of Rockville Centre. A high point of the course, for me, was a talk given by Father Dolan and Sister Julie Houser. They explained how they worked and prayed together and were involved in bringing the healing presence of Jesus to the sick who were in need of him. I wanted to know more. . . .

The following year I taught in high school and found that I had extra time. Father Dolan and Sister Julie were visiting the patients at LaGuardia Hospital in Forest Hills on a weekly basis and I asked if I could join them. I began to work with them one day a week for three hours.

We began by praying together for the people we had met the week before and for those we were about to visit. We prayed for their specific needs, asking the Lord to touch them through us with his healing power.

When we arrived at the hospital we talked with each patient, bed to bed, prayed with many, and offered Jesus' presence in the sacraments of the Eucharist and penance. We prayed, too, for those who were dying, as we tried to touch all who were lonely and in pain. It is a tremendous privilege to be a part of a person's reconciliation with God.

LaGuardia Hospital is within the confines of Our Lady Queen of Martyrs Parish. The parish also includes Parkway Hospital and three nursing homes. In January 1975, Father Francis Mulhall, the parish administrator, saw that there was a need for a full-time person who would minister to the hospital patients and the residents of the nursing homes, as well as to those parishioners who were confined to their homes because of illness or age. I applied for the position and was accepted. And so in August I began my work as Coordinator of the Pastoral Ministry of the Sick and the Aged.

How does one begin to coordinate a program that aims to meet such unique pastoral needs? First the needs must be determined. A visiting program was established through the social action committee of the parish council. Through it many willing members of the parish community are able to reach out to those among them in need. Extraordinary ministers of the Eucharist bring Communion to the homes, thus assuring the sick and the aged that they are, as they have always been, very much a part of the parish community.

In the hospital there are always patients to be welcomed and informed about the Catholic pastoral care that is available to them. Informal education of the hospital staff about the pastoral needs of the Catholic patients is another area of concern. The parish priests visit daily to meet the needs of patients who desire to receive the sacraments of reconciliation or anointing of the sick. Communion is distributed to each patient who wishes to receive. Groups of ministers gather together weekly to pray and minister to the needs of the sick in the hospitals. It is a humbling experience to realize that the Lord is working through us as he touches people's lives.

New admissions to the nursing homes are also welcomed and informed about Catholic pastoral care. Extraordinary ministers enable each resident to receive Communion at least once a week and volunteers coordinate liturgical functions for Catholic patients who are able to attend. Communal celebrations of the anointing of the sick have taken place in the nursing homes and in the parish.

As I reflect on the months spent in Our Lady Queen of Martyrs, I think of the existing network of priests, religious and lay men and women who attempt to bring the Lord's healing presence to those who need him. It is the Lord who works through us, the people who minister, and those to whom we minister. His concern binds us as the members of his body serve one another.

There are occupational hazards. It is not easy to enter into the pain, the loneliness, the isolation of another without having that same pain touch the deepest part of ourselves. But the Lord's healing power touches us and those we serve. And together we can have the courage and the openness to pray, "Come, Lord Jesus. Come to all of us in need of you."

Mr. Bruno Pizzimenti is a native of south Brooklyn and a pastoral minister at the Congress Nursing Home.

Many times in the past I have been asked by friends, religious as well as lay: "How did you get involved in the ministry of service to the sick and the aged?" This question sounds so strange to the ears of one who has always felt a deep love and respect for the elderly, even from early boyhood, when he shared with venerable grandparents their love and care and heartfelt concern during his growing years.

God was surely intervening in my life when I first became aware of a "call" to minister to my own aging and ailing father's needs in his year of suffering just before his death. The close contact which this need required of me caused us both to share in a love which neither of us had ever experienced before.

Shortly after his passing, God "called" again, and this time his voice rang out unmistakably clear, for in a local church bulletin passed on to me by a prayer-group friend, I read a notice, or, more accurately, a pitiful plea for love and companionship emanating from the Congress Nursing Home in Brooklyn, N.Y.

I could not resist, and I answered gladly to the person whose arms were outstretched supplicatingly to Christ. This event occurred in the fall of 1973 and marked the beginning of my true apostolate in the service of Jesus. Since then, through the grace of the Holy Spirit, the ministry has grown with a remarkable increase in the number serviced.

From the very beginning I became aware of the utter loneliness and feelings of rejection and abandonment among the residents.

The only "technique" I know is to bring the love with which Jesus healed the sick in his ministry. I feel that this love of Jesus will bring hope and light to their spirits. I pray with those who want to share prayer. In the day rooms we have a prayer service. The residents love the service which is attended by people of all faiths.

God's love is the healing factor, the therapy which restores, renews and sparks trust, hope and confidence. I enjoy visiting my friends at Congress Nursing Home. We share such beautiful moments together. We swap stories about the latest crisis in our city and sometimes argue about politics.

My own spirituality is of primary concern in my life. I feel that I must be open to the movement of the Spirit within me if I hope to be an effective pastoral minister. The Lord is teaching me, mostly through those whom he has sent me to serve.

Sister Catherine Bott, O.P., the manager of the pastoral care program at St. Mary Star of the Sea in Far Rockaway, N.Y., calls the people in the nursing homes her "special parishioners."

I have been a member of the Amityville Dominicans for many years, and, as such, have committed myself, my talents and my potential to the person of Jesus and of his Church. Just as the Church carries on the mission of Christ to serve all men, my religious community has scrutinized contemporary human needs and has encouraged each of us to seek out the particular ministry to which we are led by the Spirit.

I had been contentedly working in education for thirty years, but during the past fifteen summers I had also been doing volunteer work in a hospital, and there I saw a need. I felt that I had gifts from God that would qualify me to serve that need and so I chose to change my apostolate from education to pastoral care of the sick and the elderly. The path to the parish of my ministry was completely Spirit-directed, and one year ago I became the Director of Pastoral Care of the Sick and Elderly in the parish of St. Mary Star of the Sea,

Far Rockaway. This is a unique parish indeed. Nowhere else in the diocese is there such a concentration of the elderly; within the confines of this parish there are fourteen extended care facilities—nursing homes, health-related facilities and homes for adults. There is also one general hospital.

My role is to try to coordinate the religious activities in these various places, to direct the program of lay pastoral care, and to fulfill as well as I can the duties of a sister-visitor. It is an "impossible dream" to be adequate in all these areas, but each day brings its own gift of time to do what I can to bring Jesus to the sick, the aged, the lonely and the tired. I have the extreme good fortune to work with four of the finest priests in the Brooklyn diocese. Their dedication to the people of God is evident in all their activities. All four are completely involved in their priestly ministry. This includes daily visits to the sick in St. John's Episcopal Hospital. Each priest is the assigned chaplain to two of the residences for the elderly, and each has regular celebrations of the liturgy for these, his "special parishioners." How each of them relates to the old people is a joy to behold.

One of my functions is to coordinate these liturgies into the schedules of the residences and to arrange for the communal as well as individual reception of the sacrament of the sick. As I accompany the priest on these occasions, I am ever more aware of the joy that religion brings to the elderly and the deep significance of prayer to those who are preparing for their journey into eternity. The lay pastoral team of this parish includes twenty extraordinary ministers of the Eucharist who bring Christ every Sunday morning to the elderly. Each week generous teenagers are on hand to gather the Catholics together, to push the wheelchairs and to prepare the Catholics to view Mass on TV while awaiting the lay ministers with the Eucharist. In addition to these two groups, there are other dedicated parishioners who act as pastoral visitors and visit the nursing homes on a regular basis to bring the friendship, the joy and the love of Christ to all the residents no matter what their religion may be. From time to time we prepare a series of in-service lectures and discussions for them.

My own day is very full: cluster contacts and local community meetings, as well as meetings with groups concerned for the aging. New contacts are constantly being made. Lately I have been invited to attend staff meetings in some of the residences. I am ever more aware that those in the administration of the various facilities, while they do not share our religious beliefs, consider us (the priests, myself and the pastoral team) to be a vital part of the lives of the aged, especially in the light of the concept of total care.

I see unlimited opportunities to use my time and talents to let the Spirit into my life and to let him "run the show." He takes me to the people who need me. He allows me to make Jesus present to the sick and the elderly. A few minutes of spontaneous prayer, the recitation of the rosary with one of the residents or more often with a group, seasonal prayer services—these are a part of my ministry. For many of the sick, the elderly and the handicapped, listening is a source of comfort. Advent services, Lenten services, and special seasonal services are prayerfully celebrated. In many cases these will be conducted by the residents themselves.

Jesus is present in the parish of St. Mary Star of the Sea. He is with us in the hospital and with the folks in the nursing homes and other residences. He is as truly present as he was when he walked this earth. He alone shows us how to make him present and alive to the people whom we serve.

Sister Julie Houser, C.S.J., full-time teacher, volunteer pastoral minister and part of the Catholic Charities' Teaching Team, is a witness to the realities of the Lord in her life.

Through the sick, Jesus has led me to a profound realization of his presence, the reality of his power to heal in his sacraments, and the need he has of each of us in his body to use our own uniqueness to bring salvation to those he loves deeply. What began as a day of prayer and visiting people in a hospital has become for me one of the most powerful realities in my life.

Almost three years ago, as a development of and in response to shared prayer, the sacraments and personal reflections, Father Dolan and I decided to reach out one afternoon a week to visit the sick in a particular hospital. The selection of LaGuardia Hospital was discerned in prayer and personal visitation of a few institutions. Having had favorable memories of hospital visiting as a young sister in St. Joseph's, Far Rockaway, I sensed in myself a disposition and natural gifts to help the sick. I had thoroughly enjoyed my summer work there and experienced a novice's first sense of satisfaction in the ministry. With these dispositions, I approached my visit to LaGuardia Hospital.

Each Monday afternoon, Father Dolan and I met at Our Lady Queen of Martyrs Church where we shared prayer. Then we left with Father carrying the Blessed Sacrament and drove to the hospital. We checked the critical lists in the nurses' office—so as not to omit any anointings—and began visiting bed to bed on each floor. Initially, I made a list of patients wishing to receive the sacraments. Father took care of these and I prayed with others. As the need quickly developed, permission was granted and I was commissioned an extraordinary minister of the Eucharist on the anniversary day of my baptism—the significance of which I cherish.

So many factors entered into a growing awareness of Jesus working through us. We prayed each week that Jesus would take us to the sick, to each person he wanted to minister to that afternoon. I found myself trying to be conscious of this by being more prayerful, attentive to the spoken and unspoken words of the patients, and even to a realization of a real "listening with the heart" approach. I found my own heart growing, becoming more compassionate, more gentle and really caring.

My human failing of judging people on first sight by classifying them into types began to fail on most occasions as people I least expected to do so opened up to the Lord. For the first time, perhaps, I was beginning to see the real beauty in each one's uniqueness. Through this realization, I really believe that we are, each of us in our own uniqueness, the continuation of Jesus' life on earth. He ministered, healed and really cared for the sick, the underprivileged and the poor of his day. The Gospels are filled with this witness. Jesus promised that his yoke would be easy and his burden light—if we would just come to him. Who is he in this world but us? With this realization, Jesus became the Lord of my life and I felt the responsibility of making him present to others.

I have found that pastoral visitation of the sick also requires of the minister a real faith and personal appreciation of the sacraments. The sacrament of penance has become Jesus' special presence to heal in me all the darkness he allows me to see in myself—the instances where my living of life differs from the example of Jesus.

The privilege of carrying Jesus to the sick as an extraordinary minister of the Eucharist has made me more aware and conscious of Jesus' presence. I now attempt to awaken in people a sense of the same Jesus who walked about Nazareth and Galilee, who cares for people, who loves them and who has come to them in their time of trouble. Jesus is true food to nourish us when we are sick, to heal us of the weakness in body and mind, and to strengthen us at a time when we must rely upon the power of his love.

Celebrating the anointing of the sick as part of a pastoral care team became for me a powerful and beautiful experience. To stand beside the priest and share in the readings with the patient, to pray with and celebrate the healing touch of Jesus as he reaches through sacramental signs to free, heal, and make whole again, is an experience that brings to life the abiding presence of the living Savior caring for his brothers and sisters. It is Jesus today crying out in our time and in this place and to this person: "Take up your bed and walk."

My hospital ministry presently has taken on another dimension—that of lecturing and teaching. Although a full-time teacher at Our Lady of Snows School, I have become part of a Catholic Charities' pastoral care teaching team. Along with Father Dolan and Brother John Lesica, I serve as a teaching team member. We conduct a series of lectures which include the theology and psychology of sickness, the psychology of ethnic groups as related to sickness, prayer and the sacraments, and the practical aspects of ministering to the sick in a hospital.

Father Dolan and I teach the pastoral care team representing the local Christian community, the parish, in an in-service program. We work at the local hospital with the priest and the people chosen as part of the pastoral care team. We continue to work with them at their hospital, training the team clinically until they feel comfortable and confident enough to carry on by themselves in the blending of their ministries.

My ministry as a teacher in the classroom and my ministry to the sick, including training those serving the sick, have enriched me in so many ways that one ministry blends with the other, both being in my life Jesus alive, present and using me to bring his salvation to his children, the sick and the elderly alike.

Sister Marie Innocentia, M.S.B.T. has served the sick for almost her entire life.

To say why I became a pastoral minister to the sick and how I carry out this ministry requires a glance at the past. As a Missionary Servant of the Most Blessed Trinity I have always visited the sick in their homes or at the hospital. During the past fourteen years I have worked at St. Peter-St. Paul's Parish. Along with the social service work in the parish, I often visited Long Island College Hospital, and for the past six years the Congress Nursing Home. Both of these facilities for the sick are located almost adjacent to the church. Two years ago the diocese established pastoral ministry to the sick. It was a natural sequence that I become a part of this program, and I was formally installed as an extraordinary minister of the Eucharist.

About six years ago the Vincentian Fathers at the parish began to offer Mass regularly at the Congress Nursing Home. I prepared the patients and helped them get down to Mass. I would then set up the altar. Now that I am an extraordinary minister of the Eucharist I can effect a greater flow of this sacramental grace to the sick in the nursing home, the hospital, our shut-in parishioners and at the Masses in the parish church. Now we have Mass once a week. One evening each week two lay deacons come to the home and conduct a prayer and Scripture group among the patients.

People confined to the Congress Nursing Home are often both sick and lonely. I find it a personal joy to respond to their many simple needs which are most often an expression of, or a reaching out for, a deeper faith. Some examples are the lighting of a candle for a special intention or bringing a prayer book or rosary beads. At times the request is simply for shoe laces, warm stockings, or some small trinket. All of these acts of kindness establish a greater trust, a deeper faith, in that they feel God does indeed love them, that the Church is present to them, caring for them and concerned for their needs. The families and friends of the home's residents also sense this concern of the Church for their loved ones.

There was a dear old Irish lady who would not eat. The administrators of the home asked me to encourage her to eat and to do what I could. A small white potato boiled in salted water with a bit of butter was what the lady wanted. This I brought to her and she did begin to eat again—mostly this favorite food. Now that she is with the Lord she has no more need of this special dish.

Parishioners also know about the ministry to the sick and want to help. They collect books, gifts, bingo prizes and other items that help to make the patients happier. At Christmas and on other feast days church societies arrange choral groups and special events. The fact that the diocese has given publicity to this program of ministry to the sick has awakened a consciousness in many people and has alerted them to the needs of the sick.

The celebration of the Eucharist, penitential services and the anointing of the sick bring a flow of sacramental graces so essential to the sick and the lonely. To help the sick and the lonely bear their burden in a Christ-like and noble manner, to strengthen their faith, and to let them know that the Church cares for them and loves them is indeed most rewarding. It is a beautiful ministry.

Sister Herbert Marie, O.P. is the librarian at Dominican Commercial High School, Jamaica, N.Y. She spends two afternoons a week as a volunteer pastoral minister. One afternoon she visits the sick at the local hospital; the other afternoon she visits the elderly in the local nursing home where she conducts a eucharistic service for the residents.

I still become overwhelmed when I see and realize the wonderful ways in which God tells us, nudges us, and even pushes us to do his will. While hospitalized recently, I saw once more the loneliness of the sick, and I looked into the eyes of those in pain. I saw the despair of these sick people, their longing for comfort and love, and the effect of the thoughtful word and tender smile of a stranger.

So my illness became a blessing that really blossomed. As my recovery became more rapid and more certain, I saw the urgent need for the sick to be visited and comforted. Was the Lord showing me this need to invite me to do something for him? In this work I began to see the opportunity, the means, the inspiration to do something to try to fill a vast void in the lives of others, and in particular the lives of the sick and the aged.

As soon as recovery and recuperation were behind me, I sought out Father Kenneth Hand who had visited me in the hospital. He had told me of the urgent need for more people to serve the sick and of the shortage of qualified individuals willing to devote some of their time to others. It was not long before I found myself accepting an invitation and enrolling in a class with about fifteen equally interested and committed people.

Our course of instructions lasted six weeks. We met twice a week, on Sunday morning after Mass for one hour and on Monday evening for two hours. Father Hand arranged for a series of lectures specific to hospital ministry which included the theology of sickness, the psychology of sickness, prayer and the sacraments, and practical aspects of ministry to the sick.

Working closely with Father Joseph M. Dolan and Sister Julie Houser, a pastoral care teaching team from Catholic Charities, we received clinical training in Terrace Heights Hospital. Our instructions were intensive and thorough, including the duties and responsibilities of ministering to the sick and the importance of being sensitive to the fears and feelings of the patient. We were taught the importance of becoming part of the healing team. We learned how to approach each patient as an individual and to respect the patient's right to privacy. Sensitivity to the patient's needs was the primary focus of our instructions.

Once a week we visited the hospital as a group. We began our visiting with prayer for the health and strength of the sick. Then we went to our patients individually, without regard to their religious preference, and were accorded a warm reception. Practically all our patients were inspired, comforted, and grateful for our efforts to share ourselves with them. Some were inclined to share themselves and their personal concerns, and hopefully they found us interested and good listeners. This in itself is a form of therapy, an outlet for the patients, even if, in listening to their problems, we could not solve them. We were able to leave just a little of ourselves with each patient, and were also able to take with us some of the cares and concerns of the people we visited.

We, in our humanity, cannot help but be gratified and pleased when we witness the occasional glow of happiness and peace and hope that pervades a patient whose need for comfort and companionship has been satisfied. A few examples of the beautiful people we have met would, I'm sure, convince you of what I mean. One day during visiting, I was approached by a Jewish patient who asked if she could remain in the room of the patient while I prayed. I assured her that she was most welcome, and that I would say the prayer of Abraham for her recovery. Her reverence and faith were a joy.

It was my privilege to have been used by the Lord to prepare an elderly man for the reception of the sacrament of reconciliation. It had been nearly sixty years since he had been to "confession." I explained how things had changed and that we now call "confession" the sacrament of reconciliation. I explained how Father would help him and that he merely had to just say things in his own words. The important thing was that God loved him and that he wanted him to be reconciled.

To see this man's face after Father had been to see him was enough to make a lifetime of ministry worthwhile. The peace and joy in his eyes seemed to light up his face.

Pastoral ministry to the sick has made me feel complete and fulfilled.

Rev. Anthony DiLorenzo is an associate pastor at Holy Family Parish in Brooklyn, N.Y. He brings pastoral care to Brookdale Hospital which has over one thou-

sand patients. He is manager of a pastoral care team of religious and laity who visit the patients, bringing them the comfort of prayer and the Eucharist, and has expanded his team to include two nursing homes in the parish. He shares with us what ministry to the sick means to him and how working with a team is an advantage to him and to the people they serve.

People have always tried to fathom one of the mysteries of being human. The miserable, the deformed, the leprous, the blind, deaf and crippled ask: "What terrible sins have I committed to deserve this?" Their God is good and loving, yet mysterious, and in agony his people cry out: "What does it all mean?" Then this God enters their lives as man, urging them through his healing and consolation not to despair.

Jesus of Nazareth, Son of Mary and Joseph, now speaks and the lowly finds himself blessed; Jesus touches and the blind, the deaf, the crippled and leprous, responding in faith, are made whole. Now this Jesus, speaking with authority, tells them to rejoice and realize that God has not cursed them; rather they share humanity and together they share in the natural order of things. Mysterious? Yes. Hopeless? No. "Those of you who suffer in faith will find life," says this Jesus. To those who are healed, everything now makes sense —God is good indeed. And yet, what about those who remained deformed, crippled and blind? The Gospels never tell us that Jesus healed all the sick of Jerusalem. For them, there are no miracles—only the constant search to believe that God has shown men how to live with suffering and pain, and that through the anguish the Lord's healing presence would bring forth tranquility and the courage to continue even in the midst of evil.

The ministry of the sick for me then means to enter the lives of a people who still look at themselves and perhaps ask: "Why?" As I enter into the lives of the depressed, the cancer patient, or the stroke victim, I attempt to share or perhaps revitalize the hope and trust in the Lord's love that is already present. I do not see myself saying, "Hey, look, I'm bringing you Jesus the Lord," but rather, "Let's pray together and find that he's already here. He seems so distant but how can a Lord who tells us not to be afraid be distant?"

As a leader of the Christian community, the Lord becomes more active to me when I reveal his presence sacramentally or otherwise. In those who cry out in anguish, I see the Lord quietly touching a forehead and squeezing a hand; in those who, after many years of searching, have again found the Lord, I see a choked-up Jesus laying his hands upon a bowed head and forgiving; those who look at me out of dim eyes, clutching a worn-out rosary with old arthritic fingers, reveal the Lord praising childlike simplicity; those who would grab my hand and kiss it in gratitude humble me and remind me of my own sinfulness in the sight of God and man.

Then there are those who greet me with troubled silence—the silence which screams out intense fear, suspicion, and even hate. In a very brusque conversation someone is crying out, "Go away, priest—go away. I don't want pietisms." Pastoral team to the rescue! "Okay, Lord, perhaps you want the healing to come through Mary, Alice, Bill, Sister Clare, Joey or Violet." This is what I say and this is what I believe: the Lord Jesus Christ's body is made up of different persons waiting to develop their own gifts of revealing his presence. The Lord will work through whomever he wishes in his desire to heal and bring his peace. It is a

beautifully humbling and joyful experience to know
that the Spirit of the Lord has worked through a house-
wife, a seminarian, a hairdresser, or a religious to heal
a bitter middle-aged man to the point of asking for dia-
logue in the Lord's sacrament of reconciliation. The patient who sits in a semi-darkened room, wearing only a
gown and a name tag, knows he is not forgotten. The
Christian community is alive, loving and seeking the
brothers and sisters in need, sharing with them their
sufferings, fears and boredom, sharing the conviction
that the evil of illness and suffering need not destroy
since our love for one another—the Lord's love—is too
strong. This Jesus who conquered death does not aban-
don his people but rather acts through them in order to
transform, save, heal and prepare in faith for death and
life.

To all the sick the Lord says, "Fear not. I am with
you." To those members of his body who are well, he
commands: "Show the sick that they need not fear. Go
to them and reveal my presence."

*Sister Mary Douleur Shea, S.S.N.D. traded a volunteer
nurse's aide pin for a volunteer pastoral minister's pin.
She says: "The longer I work in the hospital, the more
'Good Friday afternoons' I see."*

It was mid-October of 1970, while still principal at
St. Saviour Elementary School, that I decided one afternoon to find out whether Methodist Hospital would
accept the volunteer services of a sister for a few hours
a couple of times a week after school. They gladly accepted, so on Tuesdays and Thursdays from 3:00 to
6:00 P.M. I did nurses' aide work in the west pavillion,
Floors 5 and 6. This work consisted in filling pitchers
with water and ice, supplying tissues and soap, visiting
with the patients, making phone calls and writing notes

for them, and also helping to feed at supper time those who were unable to help themselves. As the days went by my love for these sick people became deeper and I realized that I was really serving Christ in a new way. "I was sick and you ministered to me."

In 1972-73 I began to further my work spiritually in assisting the young chaplain, Father John Walsh, by finding those who would like to receive the sacrament of reconciliation and Holy Communion. Toward the end of the year Father talked with me one day and encouraged me to take the course to be given for extraordinary ministers of the Eucharist. At first I was quite overwhelmed with the thought and told Father that I did not feel worthy of such an honor. Father simply said, "Sister, who is worthy?" Then he added, "You can be of great help to these sick people." That night I prayed for a long time in our chapel, and the next day I went back to Father with an affirmative answer. If I could do more for these people, I would do it.

In October 1973 I began instructions at St. Jerome's Parish, given by Father Michael Himes. Finally at a Mass at St. Saviour Convent I was commissioned an extraordinary minister of the Eucharist by Father Joseph M. Dolan. I began my work in Methodist Hospital bringing the Eucharist to the sick. I was graciously received by staff and patients as I made my rounds. I dropped my other work in the hospital, since this work expanded to all other floors. I visit the hospital every day except Saturday, from four to six hours a day. I love every minute I am there, because I know I am assisting suffering human beings spiritually, mentally and physically. The gratitude of the patients for whatever little I do for them is so genuine and sincere that it makes me feel very humble. It is rewarding to see so many come back to God after many years and to feel that the Holy Spirit inspires the thoughts and words that I speak. All the work I do with many patients has made me a better person. I love them all, regardless of race or creed. I do all I can to alleviate their sufferings. It is a great work and keeps me closer to Christ and his Blessed Mother.

I once read somewhere that "faith can stagger on the mystery of pain." I jotted that sentence down to read occasionally. Daily I see that whole hours are filled with this mystery of pain, and in my role of eucharistic minister I am privileged to help the sufferers bear it and offer it to God. The longer I work in the hospital, the more "Good Friday afternoons" I see. As I go my rounds from floor to floor and bed to bed, carrying Christ with me, I pray to him to turn these afternoons into a "glorious Easter" for them. Many of our sick, after talking a while and having their questions answered, will ask for the sacrament of anointing. Hospitals are places for the sick to be made well again, sometimes spiritually as well as physically. It is also a place where we experience the wedding of human life and eternal life. God grant that when it is our turn to be ministered to, we will meet someone sent by him to help us in our time of need.